D1507245

Perfect Windsurfing

Ernstfried Prade

BARRON'S New York

First U.S. edition 1986 by Barron's Educational Series, Inc. Barron's Educational Series, Inc. has exclusive publication rights in the English language in the U.S.A., its territories and possessions.

Title of the British edition: *Advanced Windsurfing.*

Title of the original German edition: *Windsurfen Perfekt.*

All inquiries should be addressed to:
Barron's Educational Series, Inc.
250 Wireless Boulevard
Hauppauge, New York 11788

Library of Congress Catalog Card No. 85-32023

International Standard Book No. 0-8120-3683-2

Library of Congress Cataloging-in-Publication Data

Prade, Ernstfried.
Perfect windsurfing.
Translation of: Windsurfen perfekt.
1. Windsurfing. I. Title.
GV811.63.W56P69513 1986 797.3'3
85-32023
ISBN 0-8120-3683-2

Acknowledgements

The translation from German was by Ken Evans.

The photographs are all by the author except those on pages 48, 49, 79, 90, 91, 92, 93, which are by U. Seer and those on pages 114, 115, 117, 118, and 119, which are by D. Wong.

The diagrams are by the author and Susanne and Gerry Mader.

PRINTED IN GERMANY

9012 987654

Contents

Windsurfing today

Windsurfing is now well on its way to becoming – like skiing – a popular sport. Recently adopted for Olympic competition, it has undergone tremendous development over the past few years.

You can see this most readily from the boards and their rig. Developing from surfboards, sailboards at first became bigger and more voluminous, but some time ago a new trend started, which saw sailboards change their shape back towards the short, fast lines of the surfboards used in the water off Hawaii and Australia. There are now so many different shapes and sizes of board that even the experienced boardsailor, let alone the beginner, finds it hard to choose from the multitude available. This wide variety of choice is mainly due to constant new variations in sail design and fashion, which affect what is on offer.

Even sailboard technique is continually developing, with each new season bringing new maneuvers. But of course certain basic techniques, such as starts, tacking and jibing, never change, and these provide much of the material for this book. The advanced variations on these basic techniques are often performed with such speed that it is difficult to recognize the movements which make them up. For this reason we have used high-speed photography and stage-by-stage drawings to split up each move, so that readers can study the changes in grip, footwork and body attitude at various points. The most frequently committed mistakes are described, as well as the ways to correct them.

Each single technique will be tackled following the principle of moving from the simple to the difficult. In addition, the difference in handling between long, voluminous boards and short, lighter ones will be illustrated. The various different possibilities within a given movement or maneuver will be covered too.

Windsurfing is a sport which is really alive, offering a wealth of possibilities to everyone, depending on their technical ability and their physical make-up. Just try to compare the techniques of steering in windsurfing with those of ordinary sailing, and you can see the variety that sailboards offer. The yachtsman, for example, only has recourse to his rudder, whereas the windsurfer can steer using his rig, or his feet, or by just shifting his weight.

The "pure" funboards (shortboards), which occupy pride of place among advanced windsurfers, need quite strong winds in which to perform. However in many areas the ideal wind conditions do not exist, and this means you have to use bigger boards, which are made so they don't immediately start sinking when it is virtually calm. We shall also show you a great many things you can do when the wind isn't blowing hard, and you have a bigger board. This is to make sure that you get the maximum fun from the water.

Forms of competition such as regattas, slalom and freestyle are becoming more and more popular, but the delight of the simple communion with nature, gliding across glittering water in a light breeze and the sun warming your skin, will endure forever.

Boards and equipment

Until only a few years ago, you looked at a surfboard and were fascinated by the beautiful colored designs on its upper surface. Things have radically changed now. Today, you would first look at the parts which go under the water, for they determine its handling characteristics, its stability and speed, and thus the use to which the board will best be put. The shape of a craftsmen built board is a minor work of art, in which the harmony of its form and its practical uses are synthesized. It is hardly surprising that these harmonious and gentle shapes bring such good results once they are in their element – water.

The underside of the modern windsurfer is shaped differently according to its use. Most are concave or double concave and flatten out around the bow area, for better wave-crossing, and with sharp-edged sterns for better grip.

Sharp edges on a slalom speed board, with a concave bow area for quick planing. ►

Channels, which are designed for better grip and higher speed in the water. ▼

Board length

The earliest windsurfers were, at around 3.6 m (12 ft), relatively long. There were even some that were 3.9 m (13 ft) long. They were between 60 and 70 cm (24 – 28 in) across, and you felt as safe on them as you would on a small raft. But then began the development towards shorter boards, with the consequent difficulty of keeping them from toppling over.

These days the following types and sizes of board are found in common use:

- Beginners' and family boards.
- All-around funboards.
- Funboards.
- Speed-funboards.
- Slalom-funboards.
- Sinkers.

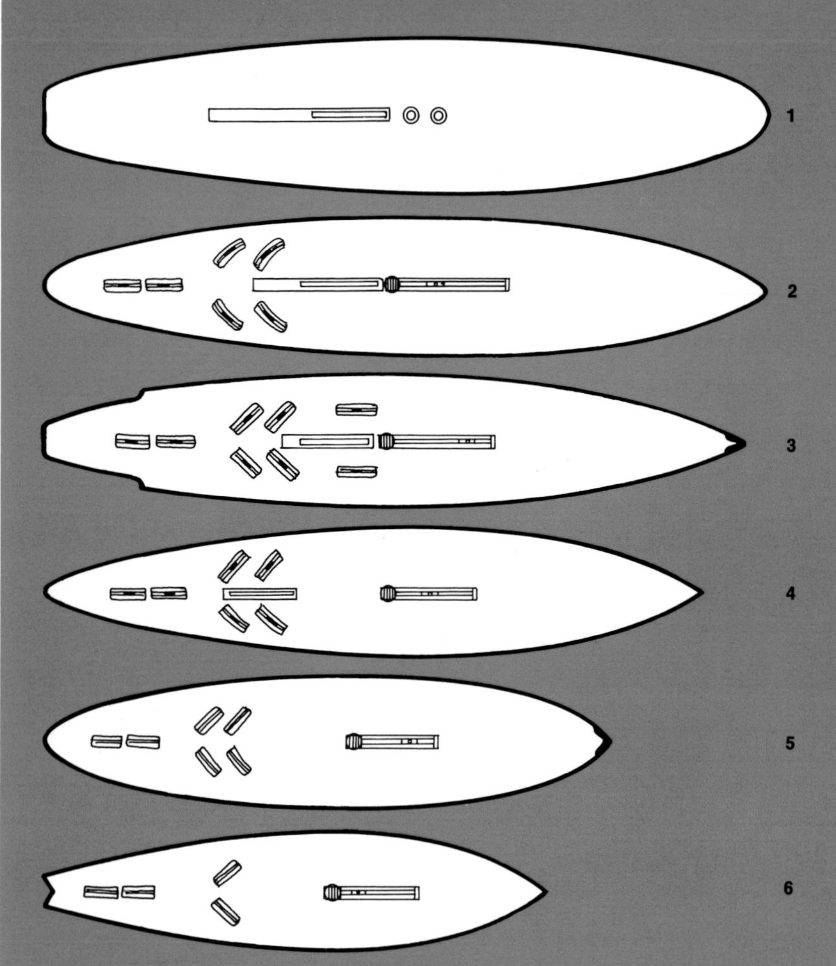

The most commonly-used surfboards, divided into six groups.

1 Beginners' and family boards

Length	3.7 m (12 ft) and over
Width	70 to 75 cm (28 – 30 in)
Volume	240 to 260 l (63⅓ – 68⅔ gal)

2 All-around funboards

Length	3.5 to 3.8 m (11½ – 12½ ft)
Width	60 to 70 m (24 – 28 in)
Volume	215 to 240 l (56¾ – 63⅓ gal)

3 Funboards

Length	3.4 to 3.6 m (11 – 12 ft)
Width	60 to 70 cm (24 – 28 in)
Volume	180 to 215 l (47½ – 56¾ gal)

4 Speed-funboards (or intermediate boards)

Length	3.2 to 3.5 m (10½ – 11½ ft)
Width	60 to 65 cm (24 – 26 in)
Volume	130 to 170 l (34⅓ – 45 gal)

5 Slalom-funboards (or short boards)

Length	2.9 to 3.3 m (9½ – 11 ft)
Width	55 to 65 cm (22 – 26 in)
Volume	100 to 120 l (26⅓ – 31⅔ gal)

6 Sinkers

Length	2.5 to 2.9 m (8 – 9½ ft)
Width	50 to 60 cm (20 – 24 in)
Volume	70 to 100 l (18½ – 26⅓ gal)

In addition there are two other important shapes and types. First there are the so-called raceboards; these are 3.5 to 3.8 m (11½ – 12½ ft) long, which classes them with the all-around funboards, except that they are built for speed. Second there are the so-called guns, which are fast but flimsy, around 3 m (10 ft) long, flat and of low volume.

Volume

With small boards the static buoyancy (that is, the buoyancy at a standstill) is insufficient to support the windsurfer, and you regularly find yourself going under. Such boards are called sinkers. But at a certain speed sinkers develop hydrodynamic lift, planing across the surface of the water and being able to support the sailor in the same way that water-skis support the skier once they reach a certain speed.

The carrying ability of a board is closely linked with its volume, and in principle you can actually calculate what volume a board must have in order not to sink. You add your bodyweight to that of the board, the rig and other fittings, and from that you can work out the number of liters of volume needed to keep you afloat. The amount of surplus volume determines stability in the water. The greater the surplus, the greater the stability. In practice, you need at least 25 l (6⅔ gal) surplus to get any kind of stability on short funboards. For less radical surf-boards you should have at least 80 to 100 l (21¼ – 26½ gal) extra if you are to avoid a constant balancing act. Boards of more than 220 liters' (58 gal) volume and a correspon-ding width are distinctly stable in the water, but they are far less maneuverable and also slower.

Shape

The edges of the first surfboards were slightly rounded at the sides, so that the water molecules compressed by the board could escape unhindered at the sides, splashing over the surface of the board and giving a greater wetted area bringing it lower in the water, and thus reducing the speed. The V-shapes which followed weren't the right solution, either, because although they improved speed, buoyancy was reduced. It was found that concave undersides allowed the board to ride higher in the water, and thus plane more

"Sinking" with a sinker. With these low-volume small boards you quite often go under when the wind is light.

A long race board, compared with a short sinker. With both boards, once you are planing at a good speed, you are standing only on the stern.

With the narrow stern you can do radical jibes even with long boards.

easily, because the water molecules were pushed sideways and slightly downwards.

So you have to look carefully at the surfaces of the board. They should be rounded in front to handle the waves, and sharply cut away at the back to give good planing characteristics and ease of steering with your feet.

Outline and stern

The most frequent changes in fashion with boards are to the stern because experience has shown how much influence the stern has on the handling of the board. In 1969 Hoyle Schweitzer and Jim Drake gave the original "Windsurfer" an excellent stern, modern even by today's standards. Then followed round and rectangular shapes which could hardly be steered at all. Next, pintails came firmly into fashion, to be evolved into wingers and then modified with swallowtails.

The modern stern has gone back to basics: a harmonious curve ending up as thin as possible. In most cases the stern ends in a point, which produces the best steering characteristics. If the shape is broadened a certain distance from the end of the board, making it a winger, this gives better buoyancy for heavy sailors.

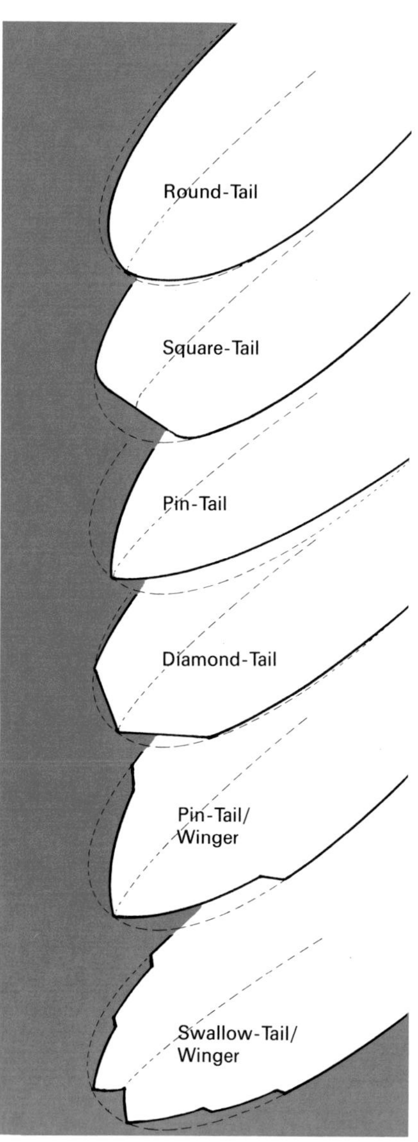

Different shapes of stern.

The outline of a board is similarly important for its speed and maneuverability. With speed-funboards the widest part is placed quite far forwards. For maneuvera-bility and ease of steering, such as is needed for slalom, the whole board must have more of an ellipsoid shape.

Important differences are related to the general curve of the board from front to back, (when viewed from the side) the front half being the scoop and the rear half being the rocker. The flatter the board from the center to the back, the better it will plane and the faster it will go, but as a general rule the steering deteriorates. A large rocker curve brings better turning qualities, but the scoop may then be so high that the board does not plane easily. For speed, the scoop is much better flat, so that the board will plane easily. For wave and surf, the bow has a more upward curve, so that it is easier to cross the waves.

Which board for which purpose?

A new sort of German instruction system has been set up, based on the individual's "surf personality profile." This profile is based on six performance categories (surfgrades). The best thing to do is to visit a windsurfing school in your area, where you can get advice which should enable you to establish your personal surfgrade. This is not merely a question of your boardsailing ability, but also of your favorite surfing venues, your favored wind strengths, the intensity with which you practice your sport, your bodyweight, and the type of windsurfing which gives you most enjoyment. All this helps to decide which board is right for you.

A precise "buyer's guide" is far beyond the scope of this book, and we certainly couldn't hope to recommend the right board for you in a few sentences. One very good tip is never to decide on a board until you have tried it. Find yourself a windsurfing shop and make your choice from personal experience of different boards. Pay attention to the weight of the board, its finish, its fittings and especially to the size and handling of its rig.

Different shapes (from left to right): concave / double concave with chamfered edges for easy wave traversing; double concave with scoop section for speed; double concave for speed, concave / double concave for quick planing and speed.

A quadro-concave underwater hull for stable surfing.

A quadro-concave underwater hull with chamfered edges, becoming flat towards the back for speed.

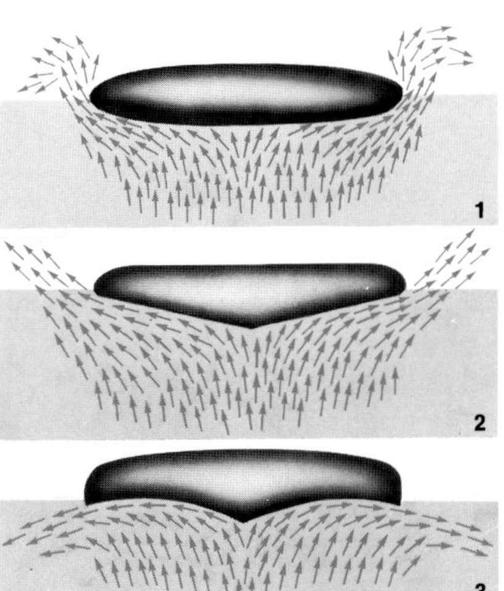

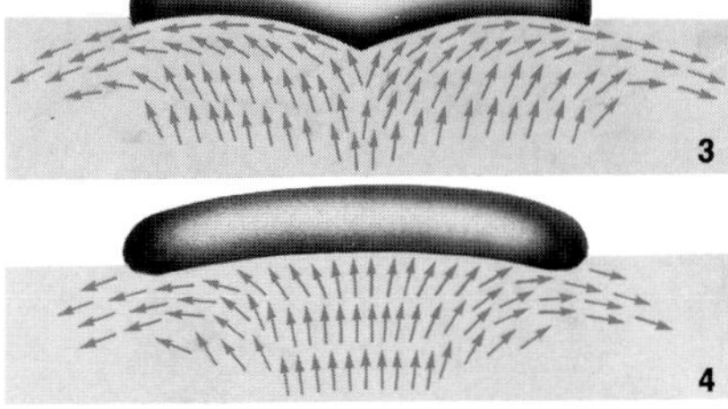

Path of water molecules with different shapes. Concave and double concave shapes (3,4) produce better lift.

A so-called "gun" with slim stern for high-speed surfing.

Equipment details

Originally the board and the sail were simple concepts, but new technology and constantly-refined sailing techniques have brought much more attention to detail, thus making a considerable improvement in surf sport.

The mast track

Every advanced windsurfer knows that in strong wind conditions smaller sails must be used. This, however, also affects the steering qualities of the board. By using a mast track, you can re-establish the exact trim and compensate for a different sail size and thus substantially improve performance in the water. In principle there are three possible mast-foot positions:

- Forward position: for going to windward, for sailing on large water expanses, and for tacking.
- Backward position: for broad reach and high speed.
- Middle position: for good all-around performance.

The track should be easy to use, possibly by means of a lever, which can be fixed in position so that it cannot be altered by accidentally stepping on it.

The daggerboard

All modern boards use a daggerboard which can be retracted at high speed – otherwise planing and steering qualities would be impaired. Since you can reach quite a speed even when running before the wind, such a daggerboard should be thick, well tapered, and stiff.

Fins

On shortboards the fins play a large part in holding the course. They must be big enough to do this, otherwise you simply drift off, or they slide away from under you when you are loaded. In some conditions, large fins can adversely affect the board's ability to stay on course. So some of the highly maneuverable boards are equipped with three fins, the two extra ones being smaller, and forming a triangle with the large one. Thus equipped, the board will hold its course even on tight curves.

Spin-out

When sailing on the wind, there are strong lateral forces working on the sail, and it is above all the fins which must absorb most of these sideways forces if the board is to continue to move forward. For a time, you can be sailing on the fins alone for instance, when the board crosses a wave at speed, and there is daylight between the water and the underside of the board.

At such times, even the stiffest and most well-profiled fins are not sufficient, and a spin-out starts. This happens partly because air bubbles build up beneath the board and flow around the fin, but mainly because of so-called cavitations: air bubbles which gather around the fin blade, causing turbulence, and thus creating a rip current and a sudden sideways lurch of the board. Tests have shown that the high-speed flow on the fins only allows the turbulence zone to spread out to the rear, and not to the front. This is why modern fins are arrowed forward:

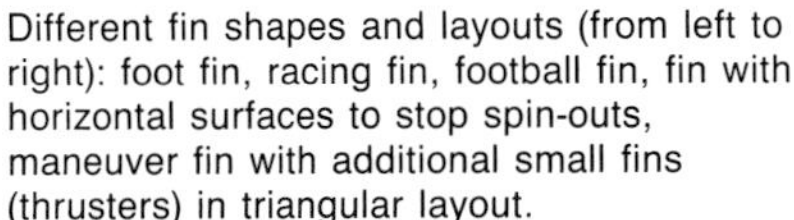

Different fin shapes and layouts (from left to right): foot fin, racing fin, football fin, fin with horizontal surfaces to stop spin-outs, maneuver fin with additional small fins (thrusters) in triangular layout.

Channels running inwards for high speed and grip.

Important for safety: the correct adjustment of foot straps.

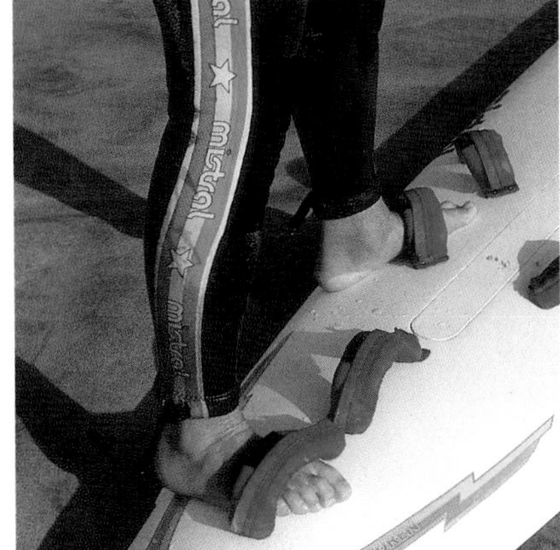

not protruding much at the rear. They have more area forward, then taper back in various shapes to a point at the rear. Typically following this principle are the so-called foot fin and the football fin, which are illustrated here, with other modern shapes.

Foot straps

Foot straps are to a funboard what the steering wheel is to a car. Having your feet firmly in a particular place allows you to use foot steering, but foot straps should be precisely adjustable.

N.B.

- Adjust foot straps so that you can slide your feet in easily.
- Do not, however, insert your foot further than the start of the instep, so that in an emergency it can be quickly pulled out.

The rig

Until a short time ago, the experts paid most attention to the board and its correct shaping. Now it is the rig that is uppermost in developmental thinking. Tough profile masts, fully battened, with special sails reinforced with plastics and equipped with all kinds of trimming mechanisms may seem to be an unnecessary expense: practice proves the contrary.

Originally, you had sails which seemed to be more wind traps than means of propulsion, and soon had you heading for the shore to give your aching forearms a rest. Now you can sail for hours in the strongest winds, using light, energy-saving sails. This is why all the expense on development is fully justified.

New, special lightweight plastics have turned the traditional triangular sail into a semi-stiff aerofoil rig, shaped for optimum performance. In fact, the profile itself is not as important as keeping that profile stable. We know that the effectiveness of any sail is decided by the first third behind the mast. Concentrating on that vital zone, using variously flexible reinforcing battens, ways have been found to stop any wind from pushing the belly of the sail out of shape.

The new generation of sails, with full length battens. This provides a better sail profile, which keeps its shape even in the strongest of winds.

Take care over the following steps when rigging:

- Insert the mast. Fix the wishbone boom. Tension the luff and the outhaul.
- Insert the battens and tension them.
- Take any creases out of the luff, and finally tension the leech, using the outhaul (leech) line.

Some people attach the wishbone boom somewhat lower to the mast, usually at shoulder height but not normally above chin level. This lower fixing of the boom is particularly useful for water starts, but it is a matter of personal preference.

For trimming at the tack and the clew, use "blocks," which fulfill the function of pulleys in cutting down the effort involved in tensioning the sail.

Sail types

There is an incredible selection of sail types and shapes on the market, but for practical purposes we can break them down into two groups:

- Profiles for speed.
- Profiles for good handling.

Each batten is inserted into a plastic component (sometimes known as a camber inducer) behind the mast. This gives the profile, and holds the batten at a certain tension.

On a modern racing sail, the greatest depth of fullness should lie immediately behind the mast.

It is easy to see from this sail "at rest" the curve that the profiling component puts on the battens, and to recognize the whole profile of the sail.

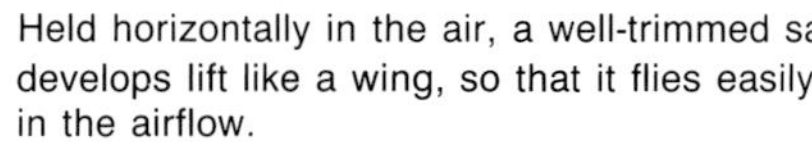

Held horizontally in the air, a well-trimmed sail develops lift like a wing, so that it flies easily in the airflow.

Photographed from underneath looking upwards: the ideal shape of a modern racing sail.

An expensive "wing-mast construction," whose performance has not yet proved convincing.

Fully-battened high-speed race sail in Mylar.

A so-called wave sail—in fact a short-boom sail for waves, with good handling characteristics. Used in strong winds on small boards by experienced surfers.

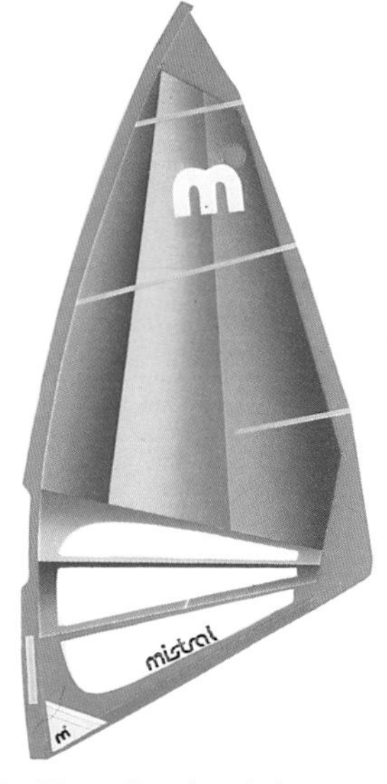

Radial sail with medium-length boom, used fo good steering deflection and speed on all-around funboards.

Speed sails

A speed sail is cut so that its foot is as near as possible to the board's upper surface, so that no equalizing of pressure can take place from windward to lee. The boom is longer, and the ideal shape is virtually an ellipse.

Extremely stiff masts are used, and such a sail trim as to give the greatest depth of fullness in the first third (and no longer, as once thought best, in the middle of the sail). In sailing theory, the fullness should naturally lie towards the middle, but in the case of a sailboard you are dealing with an unstable outfit. No matter how stiff you make the rig, it is still subject to deformation through the wind, so sail profiles with a leech which runs out smoothly and easily have proved best.

"Comfort" sails

Sails which handle well, and make light work of radical maneuvers like duck jibes, power jibes and 360-degree turns, are characterized by a high cut clew and a short wishbone boom. They are either fully battened, or, for sailing in waves, often battened only on the leech.

The profile on these sails is kept flatter for wave sailing, for there less importance is placed on speed and more on ease of handling. Handling would be worsened by having a full sail, which could act as a brake at high speed over the waves. You can have more fullness on flatter water, giving more fullness for water starts, for instance, where the emphasis is less on speed and more on the smoothness of the maneuver.

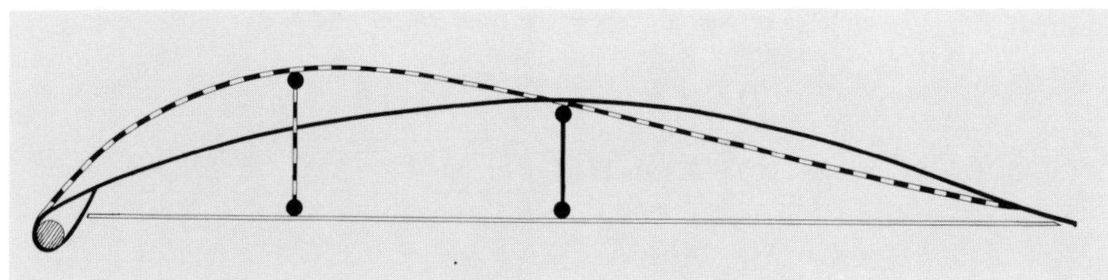

Traditional sail profile with greatest fullness almost in the middle (black line). Modern sail profile with maximum fullness well towards the front (broken line).

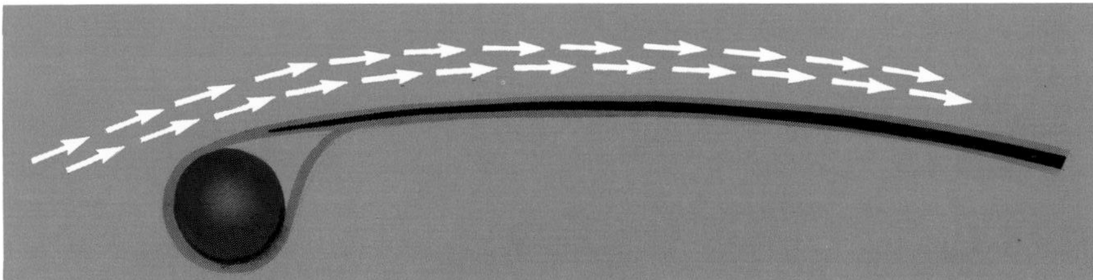

Uncluttered leeward airflow due to the way that the battens slot into the mast pocket, which gives a smooth flow over mast pocket and sail.

This is how a well-trimmed sail looks at rest. It has maximum depth of fullness forward, leech not tight, but running straight backwards from the middle of the sail.

Short-boom funboard sail, finished partly with clear sail material.

Small funboard sail, fully battened, maximum depth of fullness well forward behind the mast.

Sail sizes

In our latitudes we tend to use a sail of 6 m^2 (64½ sq ft) for light and average winds. But other sail sizes naturally have their places. The correct sail area depends above all on the wind strength. The following table will give you an idea of the correct rig to use for given wind strengths:

Sail area	Mast length	Boom length on speed sails	Boom length on "comfort" sails	Wind strength (Beaufort scale)
m^2/ft^2	m/ft	m/ft	m/ft	7–8
3.8/41	4.4/14½	1.4/4⅔	1.25/4	6–7
4.3/46¼	4.4/14½	1.55/5	1.4/4⅔	5–6
4.8/51⅔	4.65/15¼	1.7/5½	1.55/5	5
5.3/57	4.65/15¼	1.85/6	1.7/5½	4–5
5.7/61⅓	4.65/15¼	2.0/6½	1.85/6	4
6.0/64⅔	5.0/16⅓	2.15/7	—	3–4
6.6/71	5.0/16⅓	2.3/7½	—	1–3
7.5/80⅔	5.2/17	2.45/8	—	

Sailcloth

The most popular choice of a modern sail falls almost inevitably on one made from Mylar cloth. This material is impregnated with a plastic material, which will not soak up water and is shrink-proof and stable. However, Mylar sails do not last as long as the old Dacron sails, and a sharp cut can lead to the sail ripping easily because the material's fibers delaminate.

The mast

For the beginner the ideal mast is a supple one, which on the one hand makes it easy to pull the sail up out of the water, and on the other hand gives the whole rig a kind of self-absorbing characteristic. This means that in sudden squalls the mast bends backwards, the leech loses its tension and the wind escapes without producing any great lateral forces. This is, of course, true only in light winds. In strong winds the profile would be blown so strongly out of shape that strong cross-forces would intervene and the rig would become completely uncontrollable.

High-speed sails with good profiles need a specially stiff mast. There is now a grading system for stiffness of masts. A beginner's mast would be flexible, grade 6 to 6.3. A mast for speed sailing would be graded 6.9 to 7.3.

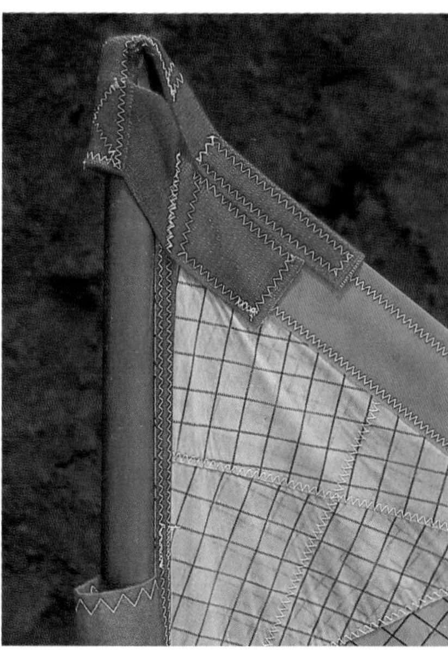

A modern re-inforced head which allows the battens to rotate.

You must also consider the treatment masts have to withstand, and here the weight determines the usage. An average mast would weigh around 2.5 kg (5½ lbs), a wave-sailing mast 3 to 3.2 kg (6½ – 7 lbs), and lightweight aluminum masts for good handling and easy maneuvering would weigh as little as 1.7 kg (3¾ lbs).

1

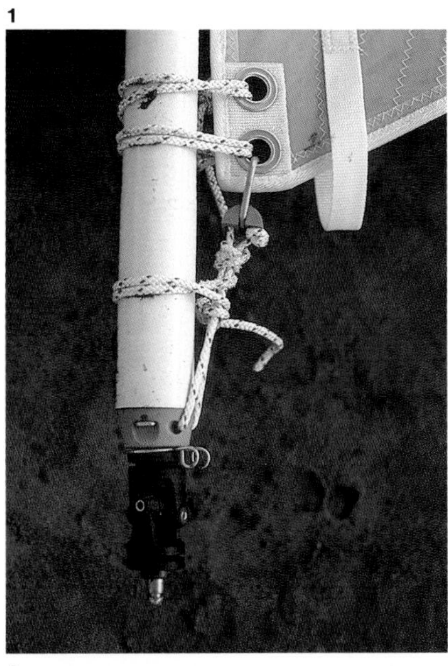

2

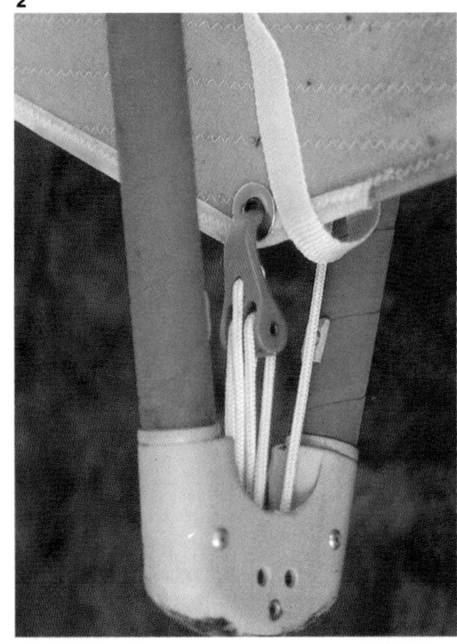

3

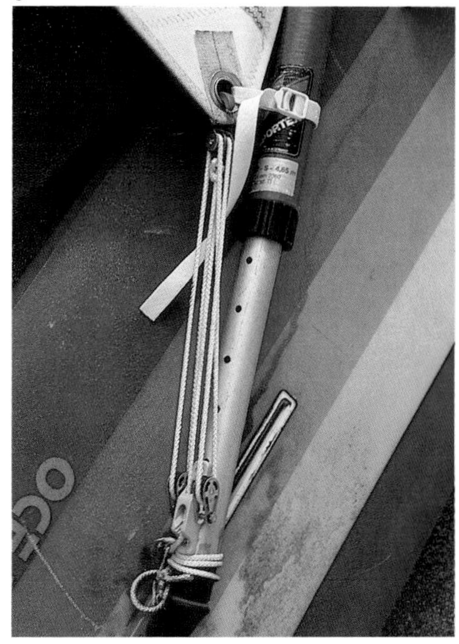

4

5

1 Tack with a double eyelet, which allows trimming to the mast and to the mast-foot.

2 Hook with double rollers, for easier trimming at the clew.

3 Double rollers for easier trimming of the luff.

4 Completely smooth lines of a Mylar sail, an indispensable part of modern windsurfing.

5 In the foreground, a wave sail with two spars instead of a mast, and only half a boom, for wave-riding and good handling.

Preparing for a beach start

If you are an advanced surfer, you should be able to do a beach start. This is possible almost always, even in shallow water, since all modern boards come equipped with retractable daggerboards. You only have to watch out for your fins, for which you need a certain depth of water if they are not to be damaged.

Beach starts help to keep your equipment in good condition. You start with the rig and board securely fixed together, and the messy business of raising the sail is avoided. If you hold the rig correctly, the board takes up the right position to make a beach start simple.

It becomes a problem if the sail is in the wrong position, and it sometimes has to be put in the right position for the launch either by repeated turns from windward to lee, or by turning the board in the water. It is worth practicing this, so that if you do get into such a position in the water, you are able to get the sail back into the right position relative to the wind, with a minimum of difficulty and movements. You need to be able to do this to perform a water start and, above all, to be able to get some drive from the sail quickly again when it gets into the wrong position. This is especially liable to happen in sailing the breakers, when you have only a very short time to maneuver.

Stern under one arm, the other holding the rig: this is the way to get a long funboard easily into the water.

Getting longer boards into the water is a matter of following the moves illustrated here. You either hold the stern using the rearmost foot strap, or you tuck the stern under your arm. You take care of the sail by grabbing the mast at boom height and letting the sail flap in the wind.

In an onshore wind, take a diagonal path into the water, to avoid the sail being blown against your body. Tilt the board up slightly, because it will slide better on its narrower rear half. Of course this should only be done

One hand holds a foot strap, the other holds the rig.

on sand. If the beach is shingle or rocky, then you have to take board and sail separately into the water. In a strong onshore wind with a long board it is recommended that you go into the water backwards, so that the sail blows in front of you. When you reach the water, lay the board down and turn the bow around until it points in the right direction.

Directing the board with the mast

You must learn how to point the board in the right direction with both hands on the mast when you are in shallow water. It isn't as simple as it looks, because often the wind catches the sail and turns the board into such a bad position that unless you have the right knack, you simply have to lay the sail down and start again from the other side.

Try steering the board with the mast. In the top picture, for instance, the bow of the board will turn to the left if the sailor pulls the mast towards her. If she pushes it away from her, following the line of the board, the bow will turn to the right.

In the first picture, the sail would be in the right position if you wanted to pull up the sail in the traditional way. But for a beach start this is not right. Accordingly, the sailor just lifts up the sail by the clew, so that the wind comes underneath it and whips it over. Now she lifts up the mast against the wind and the bow turns correspondingly in the other direction, making it easy for the mast to be brought into the right position for starting. From then on, it is all plain sailing.

Steering the board with one hand on the mast.

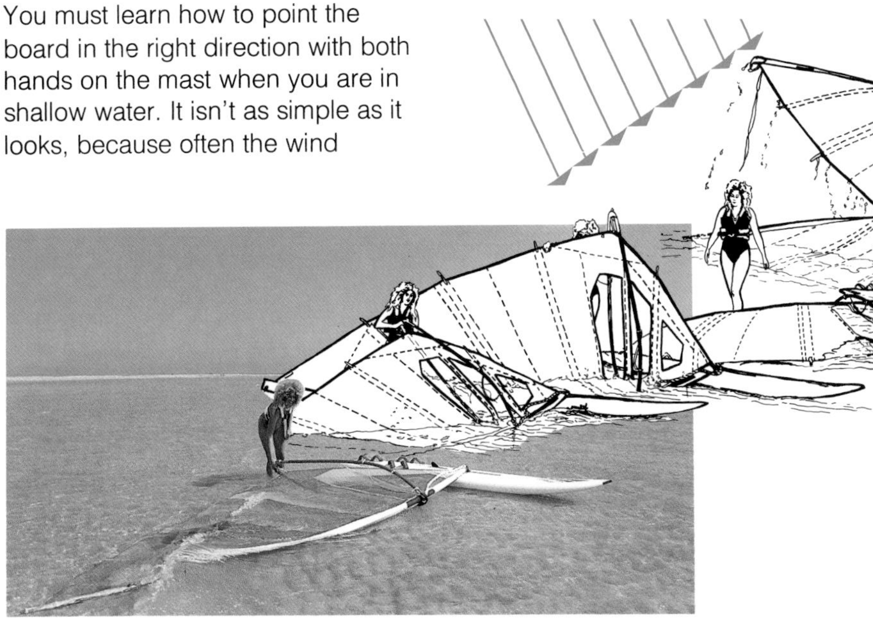

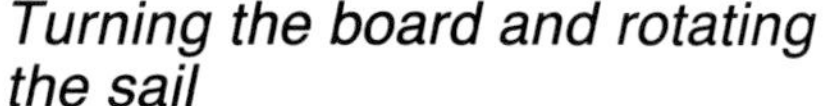

Turning the board and rotating the sail

Let us suppose that you are in the unfavorable position of having your board pointing at the beach. You are in knee-deep water and you want to get into the right position for a beach start with the least trouble. Take note of the wind direction in the following stage-by-stage illustration:

- With both hands on the mast, turn the board into the wind, so that the clew also turns into the wind.
- As soon as the clew turns directly into the wind, the sail rotates.
- Through this rotation and the steering of the mast, the board turns almost automatically into the correct starting position.
- Now you only have to work your way down the mast until you can grasp the boom. Pull the stern towards you and put one foot on it. You are now in the right starting position.

Guiding the board with both hands on the mast, and at the same time allowing the sail to turn over.

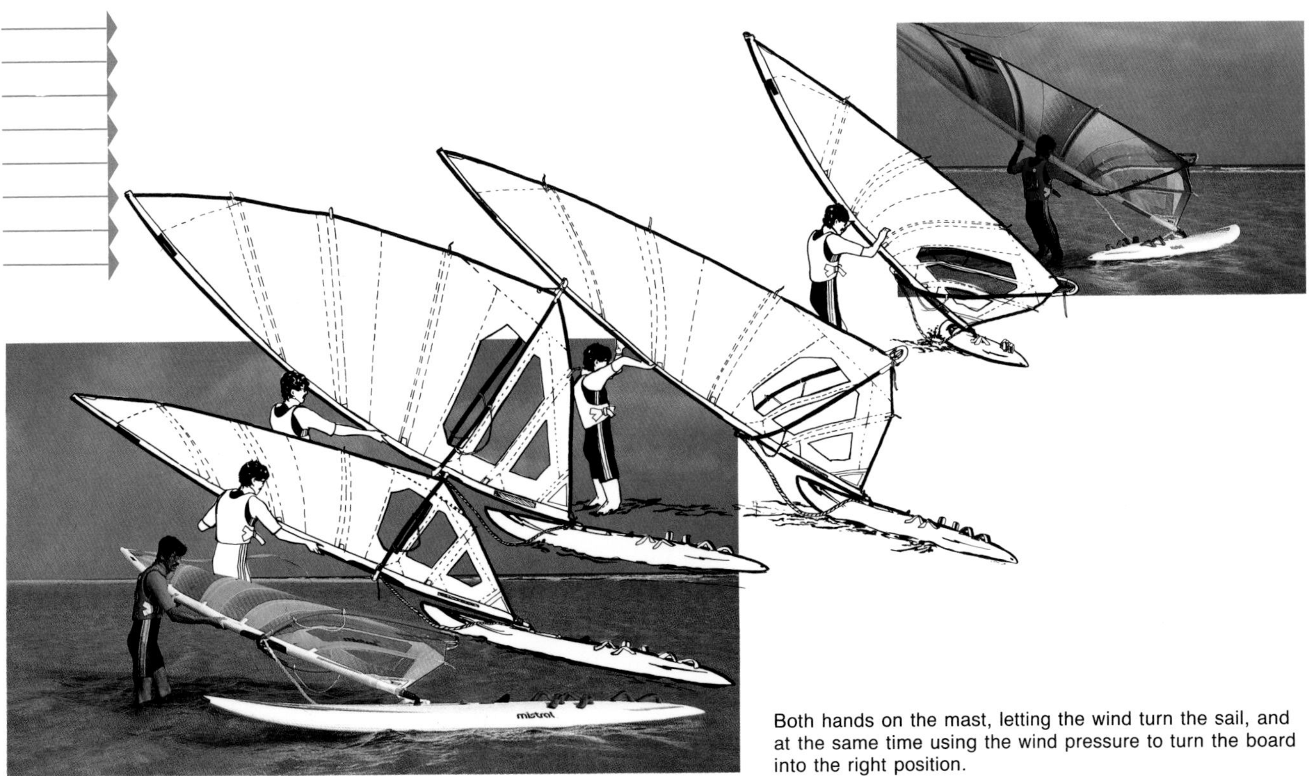

Both hands on the mast, letting the wind turn the sail, and at the same time using the wind pressure to turn the board into the right position.

Using the wind to help you into the right starting position.

Do you remember your first experiences on a sailboard? How difficult it was to get the sail into the right position for getting under way? Sometimes you had to swim around the board, sometimes you toiled to pull the sail over the board. Now, as an accomplished surfer, you should be able to use the strength of the wind to turn your board quickly into the right starting position as the illustration clearly shows.

- With both hands on the mast, lift the sail out of the water into the wind, high enough so that the wind catches the sail and starts to rotate it.
- At the same moment the wind, coupled with the pressure as you push the mast away from you, operates a turning force on the board, so that it bears away from the wind.

In shallow water out of waves you should practice this method of directing the board. Put yourself in intentionally bad positions, and try to get out of them with as few maneuvers as possible until you are in the correct starting position. The principle is to hold the rig by the mast. You will find this practice extraordinarily helpful when it comes to attempting water starts. Then you will have to be able to make lightning decisions as to which end of your sail you lift in given conditions.

Carrying small sailboards by the foot strap and the rig, seen from leeward.

Carrying small sailboards, seen from windward.

The illustrations deal with the method of getting larger all-around funboards into the water. In onshore or partly onshore winds, you have to start from the shore at an angle; i.e. the board is carried to the water in a manner that allows the sail to flutter. The rig is held with one hand. The illustrations show the same process viewed from windward and from leeward.

Getting the board into the water.

Getting on the board and getting under way

Pictures 1 to 4 show the launching of the board and the phase of guiding it in the right direction. In this case the boom is used, which can be as easy as the mast. In this way the bow is brought around to just the right angle with the wind (picture 2). Now the sailor hauls up the sail and puts his rear foot as near the stern as possible (picture 3), then puts his front foot on the board (picture 4) and tries to get his bodyweight as far forward as possible, so that the stern doesn't sink too far into the water.

Beach starts

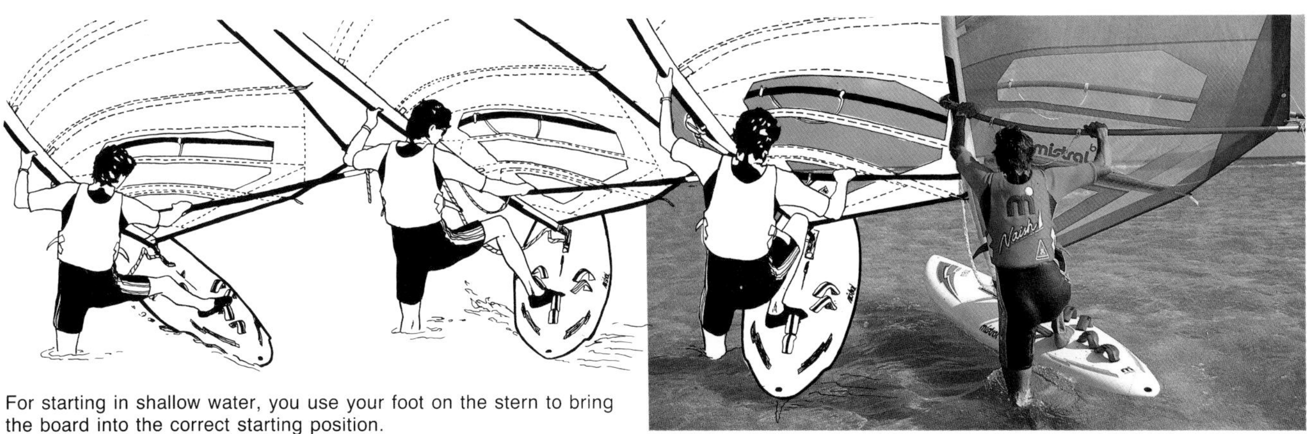

For starting in shallow water, you use your foot on the stern to bring the board into the correct starting position.

Guiding the board with your foot

It is often necessary to put the board in the correct position by using your foot. This is quite simple. The picture shows how you can use your foot to alter the position of the stern and, consequently, of the whole board. You hold the rig steady all the time you are guiding the board with your foot.

You may consider this practice simple or even unimportant, but it is quite certain that these little movements just before the start can decide whether or not the board luffs up and you have to either correct it or take a plunge.

Getting on correctly

You have learned how to guide the board into the right position. Stand next to the stern, holding the sail with both hands on the boom. Now follow this procedure (pictured left):

- Put the foot nearest the stern on the middle of the stern, just forward of the foot straps.
- Stretch out both arms so that the rig lifts and the sail can catch the wind.
- Pull in your sail hand until you feel the necessary pull to get the board moving.
- Push off with the trailing foot and step on the board, placing the foot near the forward foot straps,

Landing on a sandy beach.

so that the stern isn't pushed down further than necessary into the water.

- Your sail is now at the right angle to get enough forward motion, and you move off, sailing on the wind.

In beach starts with a side-wind, don't have your rear foot too far behind the stern.

Entering the water with style

The pictures show a beach start carried out by superstar sailor Robby Naish, going out to start a World Cup event:

- Using the mast, he slides the short racing board over the sand into shallow water, and is already guiding the board into the right starting position.
- Once in the water (picture 3) there follows a short phase of lining up the board correctly.
- Now with one hand holding the mast he turns the sail into the wind, and runs alongside the stern with short, fast strides.
- He jumps, putting his rear foot in front of the foot straps, and you

Guiding the board; sail turning over; getting on correctly.

can also note the strong push-off from the other foot.

- With this starting technique, even with the short board, he is in full flight from the first few meters.

The start for short funboards and sinkers

The start procedure is similar to that with the longer board, except that you have to get on the board more quickly. As you have seen, it is most important to get that rear foot as far forward as possible when you put it on the board, and to get a good push-off with the other foot. Your arms should be extended, so that the sail can quickly take up the wind and get you moving. Even as you bring up the back foot, your sail hand is already pulling and your mast hand pushing forward, so that the board cannot luff up.

On very short boards with low volume (110 l (29 gal) and below) you have to get the bodyweight as far forward as possible, to stop the stern sinking. Getting aboard, pulling on the sail, getting feet and body forward should be one harmonious movement. With sinkers however, the tendency is for the bow to cut under, so you then have to lean back again, against the pull of the sail, leaving the front foot well forward to keep the board flat and to enable planing (picture 3, bottom row).

When starting in shallow water, your body should be brought immediately forward to promote early planing.

Carrying small surfboards

A rigged small surfboard is easy to carry, if you know how. It is all a matter of the wind direction. Just as when carrying the rig alone, the principle is that the mast must point to the wind.

Why is it better to carry the rig and the board already assembled to the water? First because it means you can then go straight into the starting procedure, and secondly because it is often difficult, on crowded beaches, to find the room necessary for rigging up. It is best to work out the prevailing wind conditions, put your rig together and trim it, then attach it to the board. You can then carry out the necessary safety checks on the board's components in relative calm; the mast-foot, and the board-to-rig lines should also be checked. Only then, with everything good and ready, need you go down to the water's edge and you can then start straight away.

The normal method of carrying is to take hold of the mast at boom level and lift the sail over your head. This means the rig weight lifts the board off the ground, and you grab the board by the stern foot straps. The mast must point in the direction of the wind.

Another way of carrying is shown in the pictures opposite. The surfer carries the board on his head, so that the sail protrudes backwards or to the side. The board can be carried horizontally or vertically. The head is positioned so that the weight of the rig and board counterbalance one another.

The pictures show various other ways of carrying the board, in varying wind conditions and directions.

Small surfboards can be carried completely in the air, provided that you know how to hold them properly.

Offshore wind, sailor leaving the water.

Offshore wind, the sailor goes towards the water.

Side-wind, going towards the water.

Offshore wind, coming from the water.

Onshore wind, parallel to the beach line.

Side-wind, coming from the water.

The whole outfit, not yet rigged up.

Onshore wind, going into the water.

Carried simply under the arm.

The water start

Using swimming strokes during a water start to get your body closer to the middle of the board.

Practicing for water starts

The water start is the most important prerequisite of being a real funboard surfer. Apart from the obvious energy-saving advantages, you have to be proficient at the water start, because it is needed for use with so-called sinkers, on which you cannot use the uphaul line to lift the rig. At one time it was even taboo to have an uphaul on the boom of these tiny boards.

Mastery of the water start sets you apart from beginners and other surfers who still need to use the uphaul. But to scorn the uphaul completely is not a sensible attitude. For an uphaul can still be useful even with water starts; it can be used, for instance, in bringing the rig around from lee to windward, or to move into a certain starting position.

The water start can be divided into two main phases:

- Getting the rig into the right position.
- Starting and moving off.

Now we will show you the right position for the rig, and the preparations in shallow water, so that you can master them more quickly and later use them in deep water.

Using the wind strength correctly for the water start

You must often have seen how a sailor uses the strength of the wind, getting under the sail, to lift himself up out of the water.

Good practice: sitting in the water, one hand on the mast to maneuver the board into the correct position.

It was also shown, with the beach start – which once you get into waist-high water in effect becomes a water start – that the sail must be held with outstretched arms, to get the mast as upright as possible and to give the best possible opportunity for the wind to take it. You must offer as much sail area to the wind as you can. The same holds good for the water start.

You must regularly practice getting the feel of the wind strength and how it works. Sit down in shallow water next to your board. You have already learned how to guide the board using the rig. Bring your body close to the board and place your back foot on the side of the board or even on the deck. Your arms should be extended. According to wind strength, you should now feel the pull: this helps, either in a strong wind to pull the board directly along, or in a lighter wind to give the stability to allow you to get your body over your rear foot on to the middle of the board. If your weight presses on to the outer edge of the board, it will cause it to tip over and drift off sideways.

Taking up the start position, getting on and moving away.

The right position for the water start

The row of pictures above shows how an ideal water start should be carried out. Just as with a normal start, the swimming sailor should feel the wind coming from behind. The board should lie at right angles to him, or even slightly on a broad-reach course. The mast should be on the stern. Now you pull the sail across the stern, helping it to come quickly free of the water, and letting the wind push it from underneath. There is another method which still appears in some textbooks, but this is only useful when the rig is to windward. It is to swim to the mast-head, and gradually lift it, working down and along the mast until you reach the boom. It is much simpler to lay the mast on the stern and then give it a short tug to windward to free it from the water.

As soon as you have hold of the rig by the boom, and the sail develops some kind of lift, like a wing, there is pressure on the mast-foot, and the board will then bear away from the wind unless you counteract it. However, if you were now to put your foot on the stern, or even press against the stern, the board would simply luff up, turning around the mast-foot as an axis. This too you must avoid. So it is usually necessary to give a couple of leg kicks to swim along the side of the board and take up a more central position, less to the rear and more to the side.

From this position at the side of the board you put one foot on it, pull the stern towards you and let your body lean against the side of the board. The forward foot should now be kicking downwards to assist the wind in lifting the sail. If the wind is strong enough, and your arms are straight, you should be able to mount the board without much difficulty. However, if you have chosen a position which is not far enough forward, then the board will luff up. If this is the case, only a quick step forward and some smart steering will stop you falling off.

Some common mistakes

The most common mistake is to try to start with the board in an on-wind position. The tendency then is for the stern to drift sideways and for the board to turn even more into the

wind. Another is to hold yourself stiffly just above the water surface, which lasts until the sail comes into an unfavorable quarter, loses its upward lift, and deposits you smartly back into the water.

Sometimes the mistake made is to bend your arms in a bid to pull yourself up to the rig. This has the opposite effect, pulling the rig downwards, and not letting the full power of the wind catch the sail.

Water starts can also fail because the boom is secured too high. This means that it is then impossible to get your bodyweight over the middle of the board, so the wind cannot pull you up out of the water.

Upper row (1-6):
Pull the rig to windward across the stern, swim to the center of the board, put one foot on and board smartly.

Lower row (1-5):
If you find yourself too far towards the stern, swim more towards the middle before getting on board.

Wrong: bending the arms, as seen in the two pictures above, and in the series of illustrations below.

- The bow should point slightly on a broad reach. You can get into this position by putting your back foot on the stern and letting the wind take the sail. Then you pull slightly with your sail hand, and your board will then bear away again before the water start.
- For the first attempts at water starts, tie the boom very low.
- If you have too little wind or too small a sail, do not hold the boom with your mast hand. Instead, hold the mast above the mast-foot or, depending on body and arm length, midway between mast-foot and boom.
- Put your rear foot on the stern (on small boards, forward of the stern) and bend your knee so that foot and knee come to lie on the board. This is the ideal situation. Meanwhile your other foot is performing swimming movements. With straight arms, wait for the upward pull, at the same time shifting your bodyweight over the rear foot. If the board now luffs up again, counteract this by leaning the mast forward.

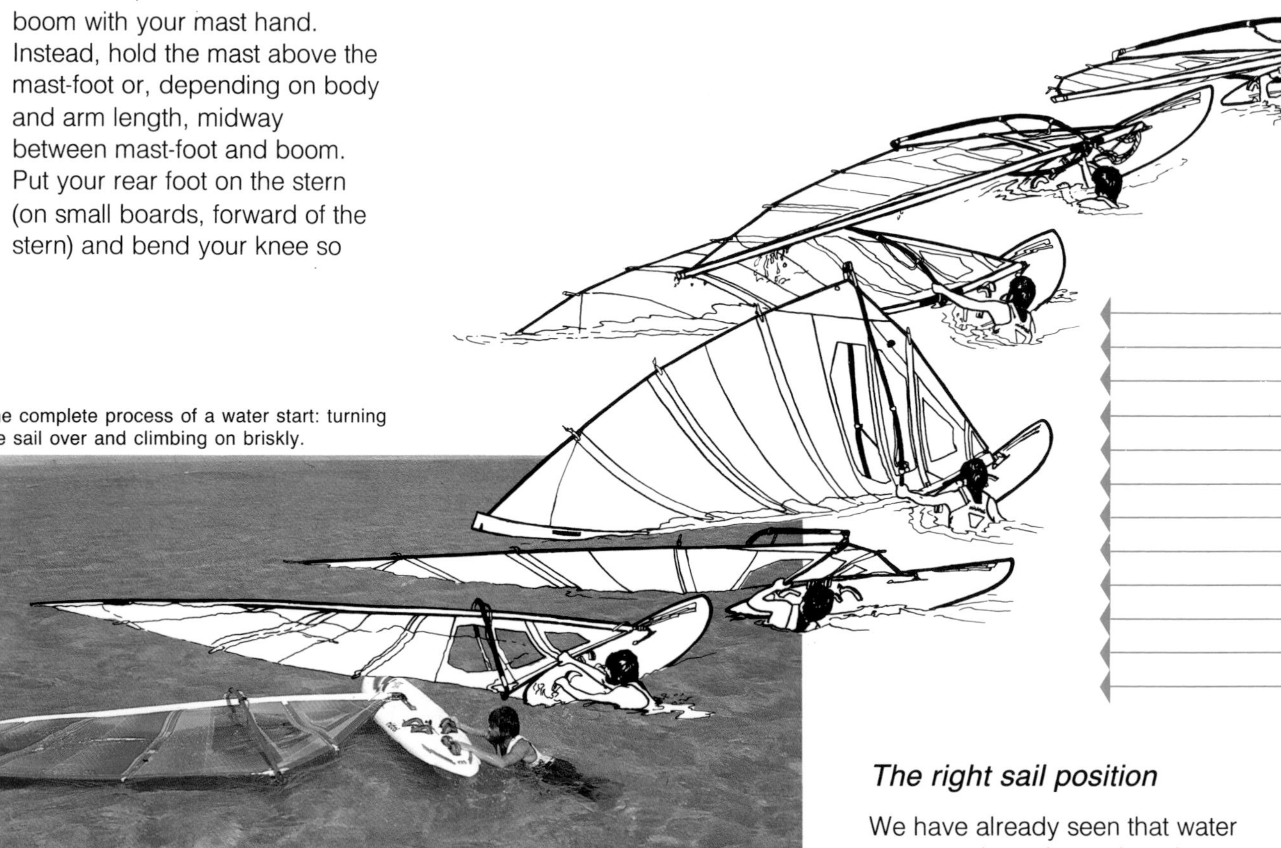

The complete process of a water start: turning the sail over and climbing on briskly.

The right sail position

We have already seen that water starts are best done when the mast lies on the stern, and the board lies at right angles to the wind. However, the rig seldom falls in that position.

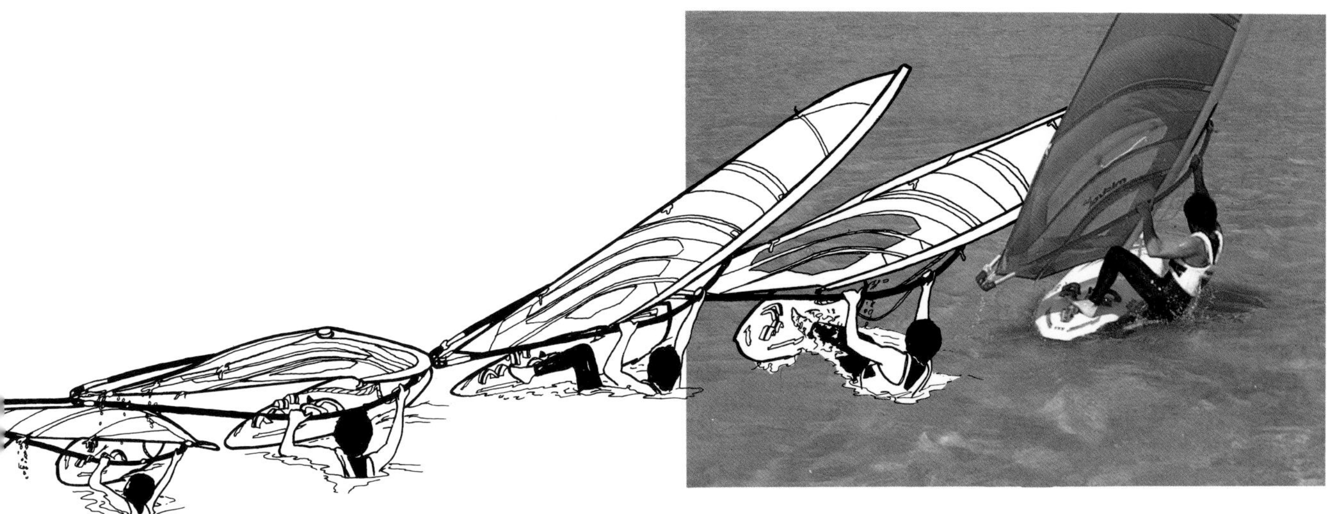

On this page you can see a picture series which starts with the sail in the wrong position, with the clew to the wind. The series shows how first the sail is turned, then the rig is pulled across the stern, board and sail are maneuvered slightly on broad reach, and finally the board is mounted and the start completed.

Study each picture carefully, and pay particular attention to the grip position. You first take hold of the outer end of the boom with your right hand, and by making swimming movements with your legs, help to lift it out of the water until the wind can come underneath the sail, which makes it turn over virtually by itself. Now take hold of the mast with the right hand again, pull it with a sharp tug across the stern, at the same time pushing from underneath on the front part of the boom with your left hand. The water runs off the sail, which comes free of the water. If it is a battened sail, strike it sharply so that the battens curve upwards. Now in effect you have a wing which develops lift, just as with an aircraft.

Getting the board into the right position, getting the body around to the stern and getting on, should now be no problem.

As you climb on board the arms should stay at full stretch.

1

2

In a light wind: one hand on the mast. In this way the body comes nearer to the board.

Turning the board in the water

With small boards you must in no circumstances, however, let the board turn over. Even when the sail is in the wrong position, it is much better to turn the bow under the sail to get the sail lying along the stern, and then follow the procedure set out on the previous page.

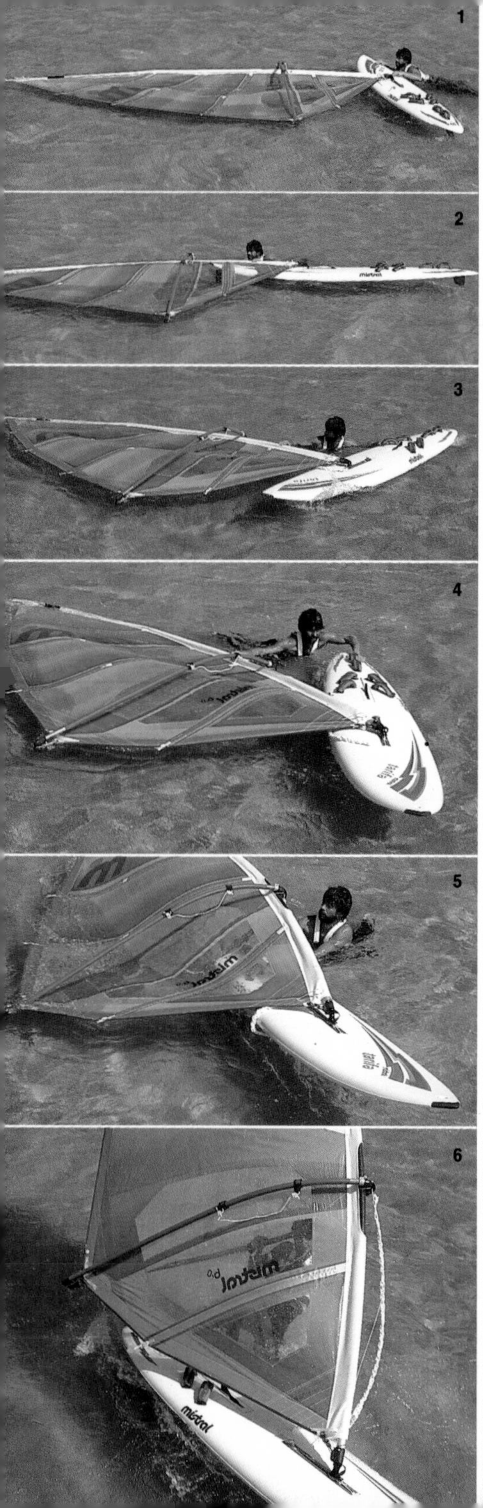

Left-hand column:
The bow of a small surfboard can be turned under the mast to get the board into the correct position for a water start.

Center column:
If the clew points to where you are heading, you have to use swimming movements to lift it up against the wind, and then let the wind rotate it.

Below:
You can, of course, start with the clew pointing forwards, and subsequently shift the sail.

Water starts with sinkers

If water starting is comparatively easy with long boards, short ones, and especially the sinkers, demand a lot of practice, particularly when there isn't much wind. The essence of handling these precarious planks is getting on correctly. The attitude of the sail in the water and putting the board in a broad-reach course, have already been fully described. So we shall deal here only with getting on the board correctly and actively and, once there, standing correctly.

The passive way of doing it is to let the sail pull you up. This is possible if the wind is particularly strong. But at force 4 or less, you have to give a helping hand. This can even mean you have to hang on to the sail-foot and the mast and creep on to the board. The important thing is to get your bodyweight over the center of the board as fast as you can, probably with legs bent and in a kind of crouched position. Otherwise, water starts are the same as with big boards, with the same pulling of the stern with the rear foot, and powerful swim kicks with the front foot as a kind of push out of the water, to aid the process of standing up.

The row of pictures at the bottom of this page shows the action of boarding a sinker in the surf zone. The sailor has, as often happens, fallen into the water and gets up again, but remains in a crouch (picture 3) so that there isn't too much weight on the board. He gradually comes upright again only as he gets under way (picture 4).

1

2

3

4

1

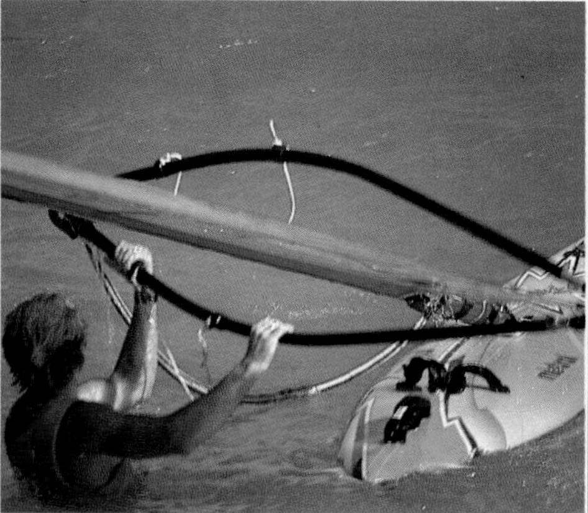
2

3

A water start in a light wind with a sinker demands clever body movements.

With one hand on the mast, come up only far enough to get the board moving. If you stand up too quickly the stern will go under again.

In the pictures, Robby Naish shows how experienced sailors get aboard a sinker in light-wind conditions. Note in picture 1 the on-wind position. Using both hands on the boom (picture 2) he steers the board into a broad-reach position. Then (picture 3) he puts his front foot on the board and uses it (4) to pull the stern towards his body, at the same time kicking with his other foot. As soon as the stern is close, he puts his back foot, with the knee already bent, on the center of the board (picture 5). He then stands up over his rear foot, simultaneously moving his front foot to a new position just behind the mast-foot (picture 6). This brings the board into a horizontal position. At the same time he holds

1

2

3

the sail tight, so that the board bears away and (picture 7) Robby is immediately under way.

Until now we have recommended getting the back foot on to the board first. Robby has demonstrated the exact opposite; but it is still easier, at least to begin with, if you follow the back-foot method.

Boarding

You can get into a difficult and dangerous situation with small funboards when the wind drops. For you can no longer get the sail up into the starting position using traditional methods. But after a lot of practice you can get these low-volume boards moving again by using the water start. You can no longer hold it by the boom because the weight of the rig just pulls itself over. So at an appropriate moment you have to set up the rig, held by the mast and the sail-foot, so that the wind holds it upright. Then get both feet on board and you will find yourself sinking, in a sort of crouch. Make sure you get the board right under you, then gradually and carefully stand up, still holding sail-foot and mast, gradually working your hand further up the mast as you get upright. Now the board should start to move slowly. If it stops, it will sink again immediately. Once you are standing, you move your sail hand to the boom.

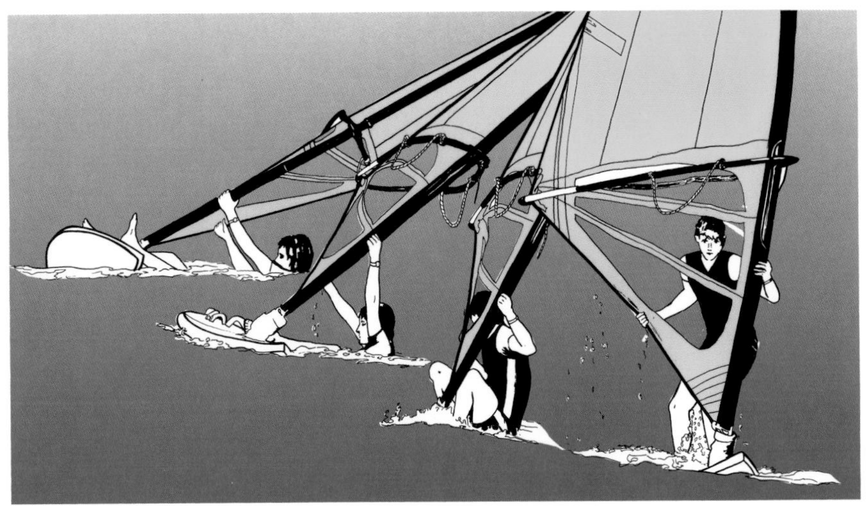

Water starting on a sinker in a light wind demands superlative balance and delicate feeling for use of the rig.

Turning on the funboard

People don't do traditional turns on funboards any more. For one thing, the traditional method is virtually impossible on these small, fast boards. For another, an experienced sailor wouldn't want to be seen in the precarious position in front of the mast.

An accomplished, fast turn can be achieved when you make the board luff up, then with a jump or one quick step you change to the new side and set off on a new tack straight away. Thus, funboard turns need to be carried out quickly. This is particularly so for the small boards (semi-sinkers). With these there can be no hanging about in front of the mast, because they would just go under. So it is all a question of

For a fast tack on funboards the sail must always be pulled across, to allow a lightning change from one wind-side to the other.

changing sides like lightning, a technique to practice on dry land:

- ○ Set up a rig.
- ○ Move the sail until it luffs up.
- ○ Take hold of the mast with the mast hand, with your front foot either at or forward of the mast.
- ○ Let go with your sail hand and immediately use it to take hold of the mast.
- ○ Take a short step on to the opposite side of the board.
- ○ With the ''new'' sail hand grasp the boom, and then let the new mast hand take hold as well.

Tacking with a funboard: luffing up, pulling the sail over, stepping around the sail and starting off again.

Turns with longer funboards

Here you can see the entire process of a turn on a longer funboard:

- To luff up, the mast hand grips the mast, and then with the sail hand you pull the boom end down towards the water, keeping the sail tight to accelerate the turning movement (picture 1).
- You carry on luffing up until the bow has turned through the wind. Then the sail hand also grasps the mast and the back foot is brought up to the mast.
- Then follows a short step across (picture 3), and the sail hand grasps the boom (picture 5).
- Normally the mast hand would now also grasp the boom, but you can get under way again while it is still on the mast.

Funboards with a volume of 200 liters and above are big enough to allow you to spend a short time at the mast without it causing any problems when tacking. But it is a good idea to accustom yourself to shifting your bodyweight across from one side to the other without delay.

1 2 3 4

Turns with short funboards

Jibing with a funboard isn't always possible. Often, when the waters are crowded, you have to get where you want through tacking. Provided that the board isn't too short and small, you can do this after a little practice. In fact the method is the same as with longer boards, except that you simply cannot afford any kind of lingering about with your bodyweight in front of the mast, because the low volume at the bow of this kind of board would just go under.

This is the way to do it:

- Luff up and pull the sail across. Change your stance to bring your forward foot right in front of the mast and grasp the mast with the mast hand. Pull the sail hard so that it imparts a turning impulse on the board, and the bow turns through the wind.
- Now with a lightning step move around to the new windward side. Take hold of the mast with both hands. After a little practice you can even eliminate the brief time spent standing in front of the mast in this way: you place your forward foot (which was in front of the mast as you moved to luff up) immediately to the new windward side as soon as the sail hand grasps the mast, so that one foot is already in lee while the other is still to windward.
- Once you are on the new windward side, don't take up a position too far aft. It has been found that it is better to leave the forward foot somewhere near the mast, so that the bodyweight doesn't push the stern under water. The board would then luff up and would refuse to get under way. It is especially important to try to get the board under way from this central stance if you are on small sinkers. And in no case let go of the mast with your mast hand.

Tacking on a small funboard must be done in a flash, so that the bow isn't pushed under the water.

1 2 3 4

Turns with sinkers

With so-called sinkers and semi-sinkers, you can only jibe, rather than tacking. There just isn't enough room in front of the mast to permit a normal tacking movement, and the boards are simply too prone to toppling over and sinking at the nose. However, a sort of turn has been developed which doesn't put your weight in front of the mast, but allows you to stay on the center of the board. This "helicopter" turn can only be carried out in winds of up to force 5. If they are any stronger, you have to jibe normally.

This is how to turn on a sinker:

- Luff up as normal. If your board has a mast track, the mast should be in the rear position.
- Now pull the sail powerfully across, and take hold of the mast with the mast hand well down below the boom (picture 2).
- Now lean the whole rig into the wind, and hold the sail abaft. You should be pushing the sail against the wind with your sail hand until the clew swings around over the bow (picture 3).
- As soon as the sail crosses the bow, let go with the sail hand. The sail rotates, and midway through this process your mast hand is on the mast. The stance changes from being central (picture 3) to being on the windward side (picture 4).
- Now a new starting process begins. First you bring your

5 6 7 8

bodyweight back with a step towards the rear, for the bow will already be starting to sink. Your sail hand is on the end of the boom.

A few tips here: it is important that, with the first luffing-up movement, the board should turn through the wind (sail pulled right across). Then you stabilize your position by clearly leaning the rig to windward (with mast hand on the mast). As the sail rotates, take a quick step back, then to the side of the new windward side. As you start to move, take a clear step back to bring the bow up again.

When you tack on a sinker you stay behind the mast and let the sail rotate against the wind over the bow.

Sailing with a harness

The advanced sailor cannot ignore the trapeze harness any more. Why on earth should he have to strain his arms against full sail on long close-hauled or broad-reach courses? The primary aim should be to sail effortlessly, so that you can concentrate your strength on maneuvers. Most mistakes, in jibing, steering or slalom sailing come about through lack of concentration, which is an early sign of tirednesss. The "breaks" which a harness allows even in strong-wind surfing, prevent you from getting tired prematurely.

The axis of force

No matter what the angle of the sail relative to the board, or the course on which the board is traveling, your body always occupies a certain position in relation to the sail. You can discover this position if you bring both hands on the boom gradually together until they can touch without the rig going out of balance. The point you have identified is the theoretical suspension point of your bodyweight, and is also the central point between the trapeze harness lines, which should be attached equidistant from that point on either side.

Find the correct grip by moving from wide to narrow handholds.

Hanging from the harness, your body is in the center of the axis of force, the central point of all the forces working on the sail. This is most easily discovered when you are on an up-wind course. It is somewhat different when you are sailing on a broad-reach: then, because of the high speed, the wind of your own speed deflects the apparent wind so much that you have to tighten sail. This means that your harness hook needs to be pushed on the last third of the lines. Even then you are still central to the forces working on the sail, which one could represent as an axis passing through your body.

If the harness lines are attached wrongly, then you will feel too much pull on either mast hand or sail hand. If you were surfing without a harness, then such an unequal pull would tell you that you were in the wrong position. If you move your body centrally to the pull, then you will find that your hands each take an equal share of the strain.

You need long harness lines for speed surfing and for racing. The body can then lean far back and be used as a counterweight to the sail, while the rig stays vertical, offering the greatest possible area to the wind. You use short harness lines for maneuvering. Ideally the lines should be just long enough so that, in your normal position your arms are not quite at full stretch when they touch the boom. If your lines are too short, it can sometimes provoke a catapult fall. Such a fall can be quite dangerous if you get hung up on the harness lines or even entangled in them. For this reason, most harness systems have safety buckles with quick-release fittings to let you free if you find yourself caught under the sail.

No anxieties about harness sailing

There are still some sailors, mainly novices, who have anxieties about harness surfing. They worry about getting tangled in the sail and not being able to get free of the lines. They worry, too, about falling to windward in too little wind and not being able to unhook themselves once underneath the sail.

Here the boom is somewhat too high. Shoulder to chin-height is correct.

The best solution is to reconstruct such situations in shallow water and to convince yourself that, if you act correctly, there is no danger. Normally you free yourself from the harness lines by a gentle downward pressure on the boom, coinciding with a lifting of the upper body. It is easy to discover that, by using this technique, you can free yourself even in strong squalls which threaten to pull you over forwards. (Very anxious people sometimes have the harness hooks inverted, so that they can get out by pressing downwards.) In a strong wind, try letting yourself be pulled around to leeward, eventually provoking a proper catapult fall and then – supposing the hooks don't automatically release – try slipping out of the harness. There is no doubt that with this kind of exercise you

Surfing fun: one-handed harness sailing.

Short harness lines restrict movement on the board.

The harness lines are the correct length when the arms are almost at full stretch.

can rid yourself of any fears of harness sailing.

In many areas surfers are obliged to wear buoyancy aids, something like life vests. This offers the possibility of a padded harness with a removable breastplate which can then be used for additional buoyancy whenever necessary.

Harness systems

There is a choice of harness systems these days. When you come to buy one, make sure that you feel right in it. Try it in the shop, where you should find a test rig. Make sure that the harness spreads the load equally across your back, and doesn't tug at the shoulders instead. It should support your spine at the small of your back – this wasn't the case with early harnesses, which did exactly the opposite. Such support is all in the design, not in the amount of material used. Modern harnesses, which are cut quite low at the back, suit the purpose well. The wide loop at the front, to which the hooks are fastened, also serves to avoid compression of the rib cage.

Seat harness (left) and mini-trapeze (right).

Only if your harness lines are attached centrally to the axis of force can you be correctly trimmed. Then both mast and sail hand can be used almost effortlessly.

Rig and board steering

Before we deal with the essence of funboard surfing, namely jibing in its various forms, we must explain rig and board (or foot) steering. While with longer boards rig steering predominates, small boards are mainly steered with the feet.

Rig steering

First let us show the function of rig steering. The sail is turned, in the plane of the boom, into a running position, so that the mast hand arm is stretched out. This causes leverage from the forces working on the sail, and the opposite forces working on the board, which makes the board turn.

As you can see from pictures 1 to 3, there is no need to alter your stance. However, you can help the process by foot steering too.

Board steering

We speak of board steering when the board is tipped either to windward or to lee by pressure from the heels or balls of the foot, or when through a shifting of weight the whole stern sits deeper in the water, and the stern surface has a deflecting effect on the steering. Board steering is often referred to as foot steering.

The best time to try this steering method is when planing on the wind. Sail in a straight line with a good wind. Then, without altering your rig position at all, shift your weight on to the back foot and press

Rig steering: pushing the rig far along the plane of the sail into a running position.

down with your heel. Even the forward foot in the straps helps, by pressing down the windward side of the board into the water. You will now realize that your board is luffing up. This happens faster or slower, depending on the length and type of board. On short funboards only a light touch is needed to alter course. The opposite happens when you lean forward to put the weight over your toes, the board turning about its long axis to bear away to lee.

This steering method functions only when the daggerboard is up. If it is still down on your funboard, it works in exactly the reverse way (see page 53).

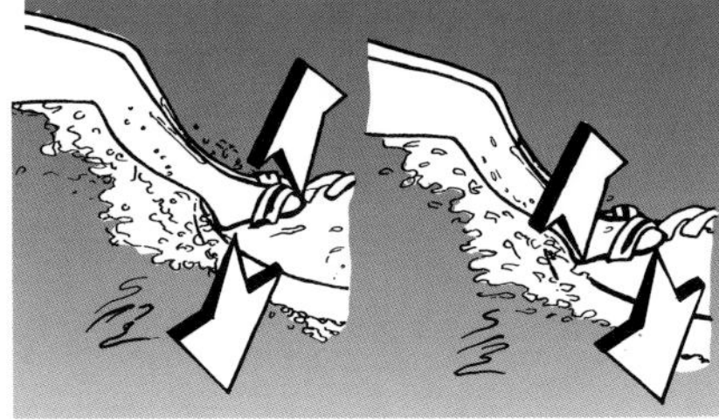

◄ Foot steering: luffing up, by pressure on the heels (illustrated left). Bearing away, by pressing on the balls of the feet and lifting the heels (illustrated right).

Board steering only works this way when you are planing over the water: when you start to plane, you must use the rig to change direction.

Shifting bodyweight

In order to steer effectively, above all on shorter boards, you have to get your body on the inside of the curve over the center of the board. If the surfer then wants to begin board steering with the weight on his toes, he has to bend forward, as can be seen from the center picture at the top of page 52. Take note of this position, which you will also use when you are preparing to jibe. At

For tight curves a combination of board and rig steering is applied. Rig before the wind, knees bent, weight on the balls of the feet.

Both illustrations show the correct foot position for tight curves: back foot between the straps.

higher speeds, the surfer leans his upper body as far inwards as possible, just like a motorcyclist on a bend.

When you are jibing, the back foot is usually taken out of its straps, so you should practice this when steering. The best thing is to put it just in front of the rear strap, press down with your toes and bring the board on to a tighter or a wider curve, depending on how strongly you press down the edge of the board. The whole maneuver is done on the plane.

On longer boards you can press down on the stern for long or short periods and push it under water. This makes the board turn more or less on the spot. But of course that has little to do with a beautiful smooth turn.

Jibing

To jibe with a daggerboard, you have to put weight on the other side of the board.

Jibing with the daggerboard

On traditional regatta boards, especially – like the Original Windsurfer or the Mistral Competition, where jibes have to be performed without being able to retract the daggerboard, the outer edge of the board has to be pressed down into the water. The dagger itself is thus tilted and becomes a rudder, so that the board bears away and performs the desired turn. This technique works very well in light to medium wind conditions. It is only a question of being able to press down the stern on the windward side hard enough into the water.

In the official world championships, in which these boards are even used for buoy slaloms, the regatta sailors are able to make the tightest turns around the buoys. The lighter the wind, the deeper the stern is pushed into the water. The board then stops and turns so fast that you can have trouble getting the rig to swing over the bow quickly enough because of the turning movement.

The jibe – a harmonious maneuver

When you first came into windsurfing you probably didn't make much of an attempt at jibing. But this maneuver is at the heart of funboard sailing. Being able to carry out a perfect jibe is your membership card for the club of advanced windsurfers. If it is smoothly performed, the jibe can be an extremely harmonious maneuver. The board keeps going with hardly any loss of speed. Throughout the turning process your stance alters, and the sail swings almost automatically from one side to the other.

Take a look at the pictures showing a step-by-step break-down of the jibe: bearing away using rig and foot steering until you cross the eye of the wind (directly downwind); changing your foot positions; then the sail hand grasping the mast, the sail swinging across the bow; now the mast hand grasping the mast too, leaving the new sail hand to grasp the boom; it slowly pulls on the sail to accelerate the turning movement to completion, the mast hand now also grasping the boom to finish the jibe maneuver.

The complete process (reading counter-clockwise) of a jibe, initiated through foot steering.

Jibing without losing speed

When you bear away from an upwind position in a jibe, the board is gaining speed for a short time. But as soon as you have crossed the eye of the wind there is less drive on the sail, and you have to make the best use of the momentum provided by the curve you are steering. You must keep the board going as best you can, without doing anything to check it. Too much weight on the stern, or too much pressure on the inner edge of the board, can have a braking effect. So practice precise steering of the curve; with longer boards use equally rig and board steering methods, with shorter boards mainly board steering.

If you don't have much momentum to begin with, then try to turn the board on the old sail position until you have crossed the eye of the wind, and then make a brisk shift on the sail to immediately take up a new heading. If you shift too soon, the sail will stop at the bow for a short time and the turning movement of the board will be briefly interrupted and the whole jibe will be dislocated.

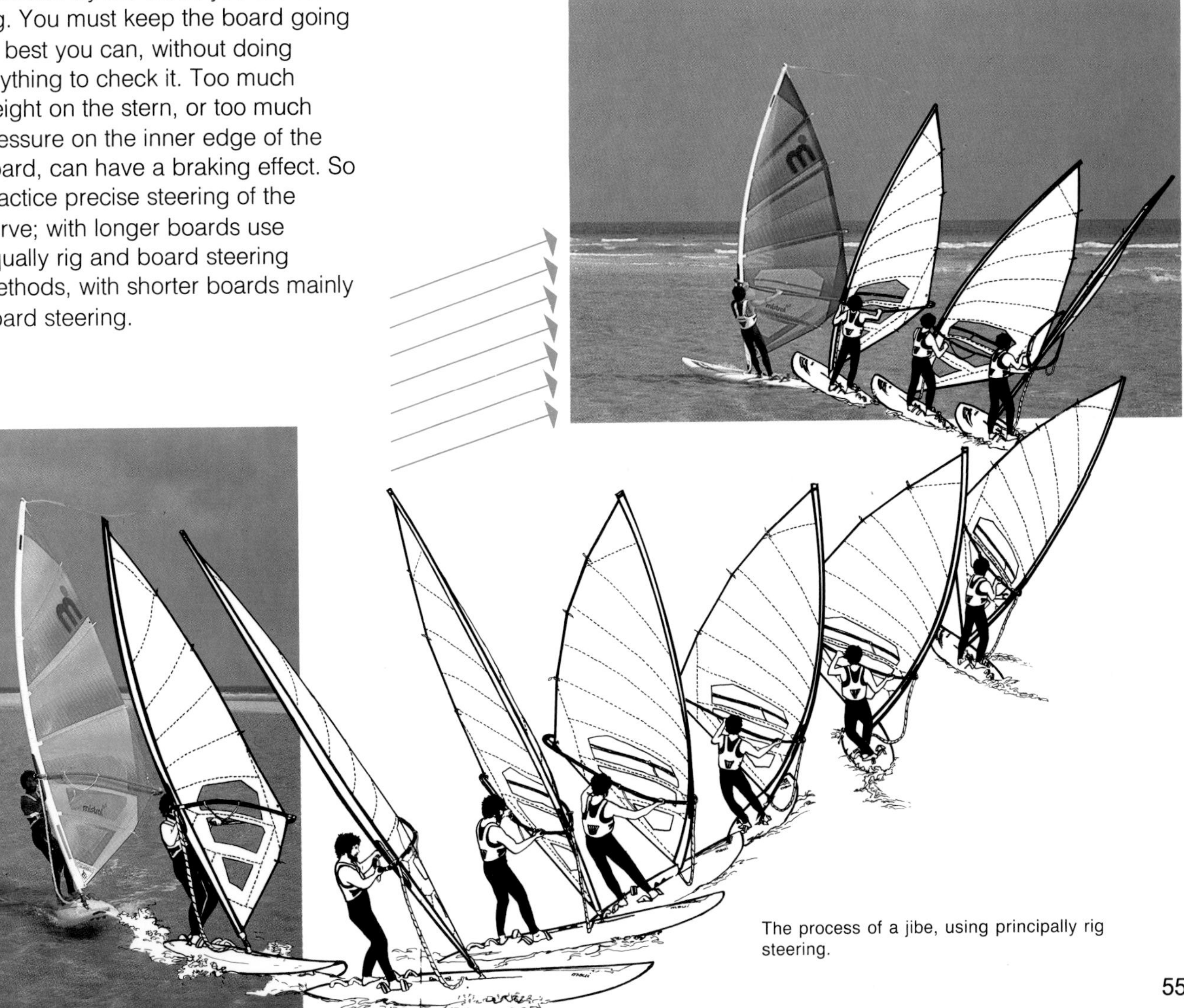

The process of a jibe, using principally rig steering.

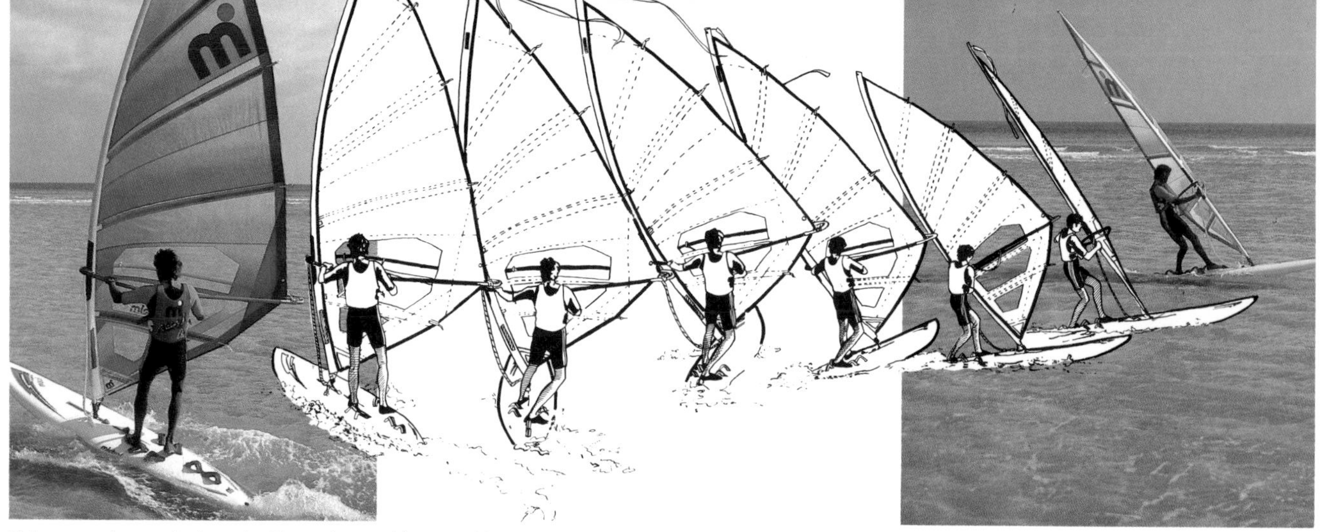

Jibing on a longer funboard with unchanged foot position.

Combining rig and board steering

In the illustration above, you can see an orthodox funboard jibe with one of the longer funboards, in which rig steering is principally used between bearing away and coming before the wind, with any board steering quite immaterial.

The pictures below were taken during a World Cup race, with Pete Cabrinha showing how to perform a very tight jibe in an average wind, also with a longer funboard. For this he uses rig and board steering equally. As he bears away he moves his grip on the boom towards the mast, which brings his bodyweight more on to the stern, making the entire board turn about this point. In the second picture you can see how his stance is pushing the windward side of the board down into the water.

The third picture shows how the foot position has changed and the sail has shifted. You should particularly note from these pictures the scooping movement of the rig in relation to the body, from diagonally in front of it to behind it.

The sail pressure point has been shifted a long way outwards from the board axis, to increase the steering effects. Both feet are on the stern to deflect the steering of the board.

1

2

3

Similar body position and foot placement on long (left) and short (right) funboards.

As the curve continues, so the rear foot crosses ahead of the front one to take some weight off the stern and prevent stalling.

This is also shown by Robby Naish, taken in the same race. In picture 2 he is seen with a short funboard. The front foot has stayed in its strap, while the rear one has been taken out of its strap just before the jibe, and placed just ahead of it. His bodyweight is shifted inwards, to the center point of the jibe radius.

Look at him in picture 1, where he is on a longer funboard doing a similarly radical jibe. Note first the clearly different grip, out towards the far end of the boom, so that the mast inclines to windward and accelerates the shoveling movement of the sail, which along with the steering deflection helps to turn the board. You can clearly see how with one foot he is pushing the stern down into the curve, and at the same time stepping forward with his other foot, so as not to lose too much speed through the stern digging into the water.

The combination of rig and board steering can be clearly seen in the three illustrations on the right. Here a medium funboard bears away under board steering until just before the crossing of the eye of the wind. Then there is no longer enough speed for steering with the feet, and rig steering becomes effective. You can see the body shifted inwards, and the mast hand pushing the sail to deflect the steering to windward. Shortly after this the sail will shift across.

The combination of board steering (1) and rig steering (3).

Jibing with smaller funboards

On smaller boards you must use momentum for jibing. While large-volume boards can allow you short periods of standing still, the small boards have to be kept moving.

All short funboards today are more or less pointed. They have low volume, and quite sharp edges at the side which you can use for foot steering.

This is how a short funboard moves during a jibe:

- ○ As you start to bear away you take the back foot out of its strap and turn the rig towards the downwind position.
- ○ Now foot steering starts off the curve, the body bent inwards over the knees. This brings suffi-

For effective shifting of bodyweight over the balls of the feet, the body bends inwards over the knees.

cient pressure to bear through the balls of the feet on the edge of the board.

The row of pictures on the left shows the jibe being performed fairly fast. Pay particular attention to the change of grip. In picture 2 the mast hand is still holding the boom, while the sail hand has let go and, while the sail is shifting, is becoming the new mast hand and is reaching (picture 3) for the boom. As the new mast hand takes hold, so the old one lets go of the boom and picks it up further down, as the new sail hand. Meanwhile, constant foot steering keeps the board holding the line of the curve.

> N.B.:
> On small boards the foot position is preferably altered only after the sail has jibed.

Power jibes

In a power jibe you try to jibe with the board on a tight radius, at as high a speed as possible. This involves almost exclusively foot steering, for at high speeds sail steering is no longer effective. In this series of pictures the progress of the maneuver is easily seen.

In a power jibe the board keeps moving well, right through to the end of the curve.

Letting the sail swing by itself.

1

2

3

- On a beam-reach course the board reaches its top speed, and then you take the rear foot out of its strap (picture 1).
- Now you lean inwards, pressing on the balls of the feet (picture 2).
- The mast arm is extended, then the sail is pushed outwards, then pulled in to the body, helping it turn over (picture 3).
- The sail is shifted, and now you can clearly see how much speed the board has (picture 4).
- The sail is pulled in, and the board accelerates again (picture 5).

The danger with the power jibe is that you sometimes put too much pressure on the edge of the board and, instead of turning, the board carries straight on. You correct this by suddenly putting your weight back on the stern, which makes the stern grip once more.

Letting the sail swing by itself

During a high-wind jibe which, as we have already described, can be completed with foot steering, the sail can be guided at speed so that it virtually swings by itself from one side to the other.

To start with, you keep the sail quite tight, as on a normal broad-reach course, so as to reach the greatest possible speed. Then you use foot steering to move into the curve. If you were now to hang on tight to the

Pulling the rig back when jibing on a small funboard serves to accelerate the turning movement.

4 5 6

sail, the point would come where the sail would want to turn by itself, pushed towards another angle by the curve which the board is describing. So if you let it go, it swings freely across the bow. You must of course hold the rig by one hand on the mast, to stop it falling into the water. It is important to lean the mast back towards your body. Note in the pictures how the body is bent forwards, and note the stance of the sailor. He keeps the board as flat as he can, so that the funboard loses no speed on the turn. Pushing the stern down would be good for the steering, but it would also have a braking effect. With a tight turn, you literally come to a standstill when the sail shifts, and you have to start again on the new heading. With the leaned-forward position of the body the board glides better, and the whole jibe can be performed with better speed.

While with longer boards it isn't necessary to hold the mast back quite as far, it is a distinct advantage on short funboards, especially in a strong wind. The lighter the wind, the more upright the mast can stay during the jibe.

During the jibe the foot position does not change, but stays where it is best for foot steering.

1 2 3 4

1

2

3

4

Using the knees for board steering

With the aid of a transparent demonstration sail we can clearly show board-steering technique on the jibe. In this the use of your knees can play an important role. Bending your knees can help to bring your bodyweight over the board, or to put more pressure on through the balls of your feet, so that you can more effectively tilt the board over towards the lee side.

Good practice can be obtained by slalom sailing on a beam-reach course. Alternating sides, you luff up or bear away. Try this both in high winds and in less wind. You then learn how to control your board in turns. Above all, don't stay in your foot straps, because it is very important to learn how to steer your board through shifting of your weight – much as wave surfers have to do. If you have to put your entire bodyweight over your feet or your heels, then you will be automatically taking up the right position for a turn to leeward.

Straps certainly do give you more control, helping to tilt the board. For example, if you are pushing down on your back foot to tilt the board downwards on the lee side, the front foot in the strap should be simultaneously pulling up. Of course, you have to acquire the technique of board steering with your feet in the straps, but often you will have to react very quickly when your feet aren't strapped in.

The transparent demonstration sail shows how bodyweight is shifted inwards, and the unusual bending of the body.

For wide-radius turns at speed, the bodyweight, and also the foot position, should be as far forward as possible, so that the board continues to glide. This is easily seen from the picture on the right.

If you are turning in crowded water, you move the sail only after assessing the situation.

1 2 3 4

When the grip changes, the foot position usually stays the same.

Changing foot position

Note how, in previous illustrations and drawings, the position of your feet has to change. Some sailors prefer to change position only after the sail has shifted to its new position. On the other hand, others will change just before or during the shifting phase. It is partly a question of wind strength and wave conditions. For example, in a power jibe, which needs a considerable amount of board steering, you should stay for as long as possible in the original position, so as to keep the board turning through the grip of the edge in the water.

1

2

Grip technique

Let us concentrate, for this series of illustrations, on grip technique. In light-wind conditions, it is advisable to alter your grip, moving along the boom two or three hands-breadths towards the clew, so that the mast can be sufficiently guided into a downwind position.

When through rig and board steering the board bears away, the mast hand should be moving back along the boom towards the mast, which should now be leaned backwards. Then the sail hand grips the mast and pulls it close to the body into a downwind position again. Now first the sail hand and then the mast hand grasps the boom. It is clearly shown how the sailor tries to get moving again immediately. As this is only a short, low-volume board, he moves his weight forward to start.

This is something you also observe when making water starts with sinkers and semi-sinkers.

You can practice sail shifting and its accompanying grip changes on dry land. Provided there isn't too strong a wind, you can set up a ring in front of you on the shore.

Summary

- Rig steering: in light winds grip further out towards the clew, so that you can better turn the sail before the wind, and the board more quickly and effectively bears away.
- Board steering: bring your bodyweight over the balls of the feet, so that you can more easily tilt the board to leeward.
- Body stance: bend your knees slightly and lean inwards. Your upper body should be leaned forward, never back.
- Feet position: take your rear foot out of the strap, and if necessary place it somewhat to leeward.
- Heeling over: when going into a jibe, you always use rig steering. Heeling the board over is a very effective help here, but don't heel over too much or you will cause the board to cut off, stall or chop.

It is important to practice above all holding an exact curving course with your feet. A common mistake is to forget your board steering when you are concentrating on the sail shifting. For this reason you have to practice effective board steering independent of rig handling, only shifting sail when you get to the end of a curve.

Grip technique for a fast jibe.

1 In a one-hand jibe you have to trust to your foot steering. One hand dips briefly in the water.

2

3

4

Then it will shift to the other side virtually by itself. Shifting the sail too early will only interrupt the turn, the board will almost stop on a forward course and you will have great problems getting it going again.

The one-hand jibe

3

4

5

2

1

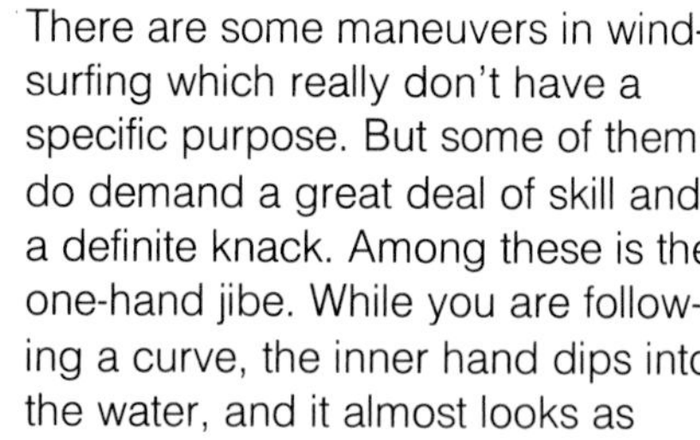

There are some maneuvers in windsurfing which really don't have a specific purpose. But some of them do demand a great deal of skill and a definite knack. Among these is the one-hand jibe. While you are following a curve, the inner hand dips into the water, and it almost looks as

6 7 8 9

The one-hand jibe (clockwise from bottom left) may be a bit of fun, but it has a high degree of difficulty.

though you are trying to establish a point around which you are turning. It also gives the impression that the sailor is using the hand as some additional means of steering, rather as a canoeist might put his paddle sideways in the water to alter course. In fact, the direction of travel is hardly influenced by the hand, but the maneuver does look very spectacular and is highly photogenic. It also encourages mobility on the board, because you have to carry out this movement with no recourse to rig steering.

You are moving at high speed on a board-reach course and as usual move into the jibe turn. Get to the point where you would normally let go with the sail hand to grasp the mast, and instead dip your hand into the water, bending your knees more as you do so. Meanwhile, the mast hand holds the boom as far forward as possible. While your hand is in the water, the clew moves further and further across the bow. As soon as it comes to the downwind line, stand up again and shift sail as normal.

The snap jibe

The snap or disc jibe can only be effectively carried on on short funboards – that is, on sinkers and semi-sinkers. It is a radical maneuver for sudden changes of direction, whereby the board hardly describes any kind of a curve at all, but is literally turned on the spot into a new course.

This is how it happens:

- Slacken sail, so as to reduce your speed a little.
- Now suddenly bring your whole bodyweight down on your back foot, so that the stern digs deep into the water.
- At the same time, heave up on the front foot, which is in the foot strap, and swing the board hard back to the side.
- This process is helped by the back foot, which is pushing the board in the opposite direction.
- Pick up speed with the clew pointing forward, and only then shift sail.

The decisive element is the digging-down of the stern into the water, which creates a sudden swell against which the board can be more easily tipped sideways. The pressure from the back foot helps the stern slip around. The fins no longer have a stabilizing effect because the board is virtually at a standstill. The jibe is not a smooth maneuver at all, and looks very abrupt.

> N.B.
> This maneuver is worth practicing, for it can also be used as a safety measure, since, especially in waters with a lot of traffic, or in surf, you sometimes have to change direction in an instant.

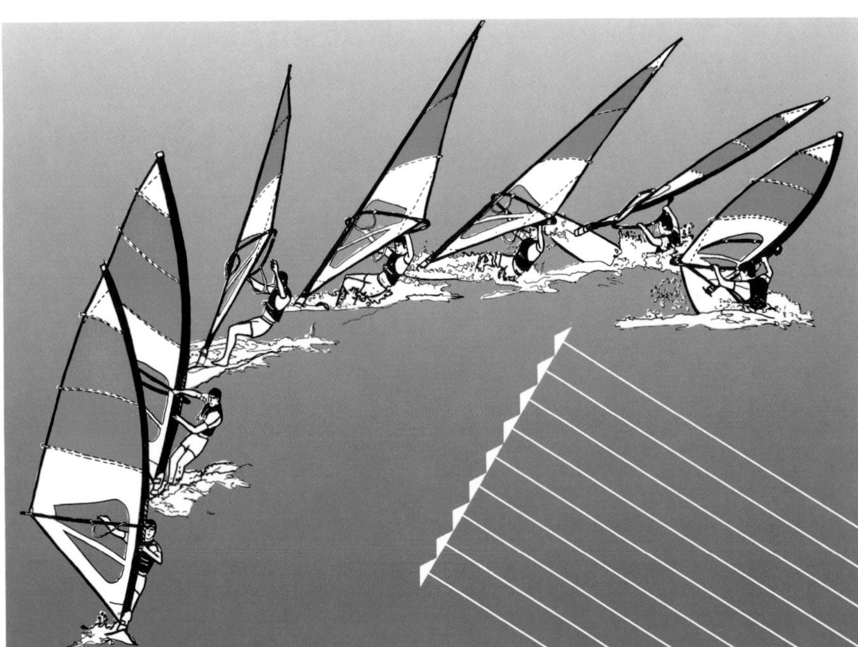

In the snap jibe the board turns virtually on the spot.

3

2

1

The duck jibe

The most attractive type of jibe for the funboard surfer is the duck jibe. In this, the clew doesn't swing over the bow, but instead you hold on to the clew, and it is the mast which crosses the bow to achieve the change of wind side. Almost all funboard sails have a sail-foot which curves sharply upwards. This gives you enough room to duck underneath if you wish. It is this kind of sail which makes the duck jibe possible: the sailor slips underneath the sail. The main advantage is that, after the jibe, you don't have to cope with the great shovel action of the sail. Instead, the sail stays virtually at the right angle throughout, which makes the maneuver look very smooth.

The duck jibe can only work if the board has enough speed to come smoothly through the curve. And it also demands a great deal of precision on the part of the sailor. The duck jibe is a beautiful maneuver, but very difficult to perform. There is scarcely another maneuver which represents modern windsurfing techniques so outstandingly. The action of the board is reminiscent of surfing, from which boardsailing takes its origins. The handling of the

The duck jibe—a very beautiful but difficult maneuver.

1

2

3

sail looks really artistic, and depends to a great degree on the correct assessment of the wind strength on the sail. It also demands a great deal of body control. Done correctly, this maneuver is the essence of funboard sailing.

The phases of a duck jibe

Before you can think of learning the duck jibe, you must be able completely to master the power jibe. You must have the ability to hold the board on an exact curve at high speed, to the extent that at the critical point, when you come before the wind the stern does not go under, nor is the radius of the curve lost.

So, before you tackle a duck jibe, practice the exact steering of a curve at speed. Surf at the highest possible speed on a beam-reach course, then bear away to broad-reach and even try to accelerate by "pumping" with the rig. Now foot steering comes into effect through weighting the inner side of the curve. This is where the duck jibe begins.

- At the highest possible speed on a broad-reach course, board steering starts to take effect, and you note that spray starts to come up on one side, which denotes the start of the curve (picture 1).
- The sail hand now slides right back to hold the boom at the rear, so that the weight of the mast pulls the whole rig to leeward. Meanwhile, foot steering is continuing its effect, and the board tilts to one side at the rear. However, the stern shouldn't be digging deep into the water because this causes too much loss of speed (picture 2).
- Now the mast hand reaches underneath the sail to hold the boom on the other side. By this time the mast is bent considerably inwards, the masthead effectively pointing to the mid-point of the curve which the board is following. However, be careful not to let the mast lean too far over, otherwise the weight of the rig could produce a fall inwards (picture 3).
- As soon as the "old" mast hand has become the "new" sail hand, the "old" sail hand lets go, and changes to the new side of the sail (picture 4).

1

2

3

4

Correct sail handling during the duck jibe. The mast is not too near the water: this allows it to be pulled upright again.

- The mast is now somewhat bent backwards, and you grasp as far forward along the boom as you can (picture 5).
- With the mast hand forward, the whole rig is now pulled upright past the upper body, and at the same time the sail is fully slackened (picture 6).
- The sail is tightened again as the curve is completed (picture 7).

While the mast hand is still holding the sail behind by the boom, and the whole rig is tilted to leeward, it often happens that you either lose the radius of the curve and sail straight on, or because you lose too much speed you stop in mid-curve, the rig overbalances the board and you fall to leeward.

Another critical point comes once you have reached around the sail. If you don't reach far enough along the boom, then when you reach the position of picture 6, the wind, which is now coming diagonally behind you, can pull the sail forwards, so

5

6

7

The grip on the sail must follow the turning movement of the board. Turning the rig too soon or too late will unavoidably lead to a spill.

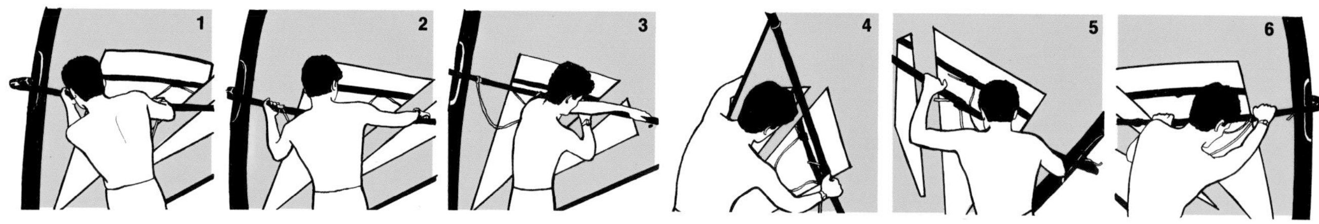

The grip technique for a duck jibe, step by step.

make sure you hold tight. It is thus important to reach as far forward with the mast hand as possible, leaving yourself free behind the sail to pull again only after regaining your course.

Intermediate grip on the sail-foot

When you are practicing, it may be easier for you to develop an intermediate grip. Before you change from one side of the boom to the other, hold the sail-foot for a short time, with the idea of stabilizing the process somewhat. This means you grasp well around with your sail hand, leaning the rig to leeward. As the mast hand is not needed for the moment, it can take hold of the sail-foot. Now the other hand, the "old" sail hand, takes hold of the sail-foot too, leaving the "new" mast hand free and able to grasp the boom on the new side as far down as possible.

The one problem here is with the sailcloth. It is often covered in Mylar right to the edge, which will slip out of your fingers if you do not hold tight. However, after a few tries you will find you can dispense with this intermediate grip. Practice on dry land the movements which are shown on the right.

Practice on the shore

You have to know the succession of hand grips so well that you can do it in your sleep. So it is vital to practice the various holds on dry land, as follows:

- Set yourself up with the rig in a beam-reach position.
- The sail hand should grasp along the boom as far as it can, in the direction of the clew.
- Now the mast hand grasps even further down the boom, using a kind of cross-over grip, and the mast now tilts to leeward. This brings the clew up, and it is now

The intermediate grip on the sail-foot.

1

2

3

Properly carried out, the duck jibe does not tip the rig too far inwards.

easy to slip the upper body under the sail-foot, and grasp as far down the boom with the new mast hand as you can. Let the sail swing easily through the wind, and then take hold with the sail hand.

Foot position

The duck jibe only works when board steering is initiated with clean, sure footwork. Just as with the power jibe, the board should steer through the entire curve, and the foot position should change only at the end. In the curve, the front foot should stay in its strap, while the rear one – as we said when describing jibe technique – is placed either at or just in front of its strap, depending on the length of the board. It is best to take up a position slightly to leeward, which allows the board to be canted over more easily.

4
3
2
4
3
2
4
3
2

On the left-hand page three versions of the duck jibe are shown, with direct grip. In the upper sequence you can clearly see how the mast hand grips the boom as far forward as possible. (Each sequence right to left.)

The direct reach-around

Here you can clearly see the advanced way of doing the duck jibe, using a direct reach-around technique. For this, the sail hand grasps the boom far back, then the mast hand crosses behind it to take hold. The rig swings to leeward, the clew comes up high, the upper body slides underneath onto the new sail side and the mast hand grasps as far forward as possible along the boom. Take a good look at this direct reach-around technique, shown from three different perspectives on the left-hand page.

One-hand duck jibe

Just as with the straightforward one-hand jibe, this is a spectacular maneuver without any specific purpose, except perhaps to amaze by its sheer difficulty. Touching the water with one hand during an already difficult maneuver brings bonus points in World Cup surfing events. So anyone who can serve up a one-handed duck jibe is certainly one of the select band of funboard experts.

Note the following differences from a standard duck jibe: Tipping the rig to leeward, while the mast hand is grasping below the sail-foot to the new sail side, you dip the other hand in the water on its way, and then grasp the boom as far forward as possible.

The one-hand duck jibe.

Correct position

The correct position on a surfboard is the most important prerequisite for, on the one hand, tireless surfing and, on the other hand, the real success of maneuvers and techniques. In addition, the way the bodyweight is used plays a major role in the trim of the board. The surfer and his bodyweight form the central component of an unstable sailing system.

Whereas in yachting you can speak of "stabilizing systems," in which the body plays a role only as stabilizing ballast, on a surfboard you are compelled not only to use the body to pass on the forces working on the sail to the board, but also to influence speed and steering through the right positioning of your bodyweight, and the correct stance. All this costs effort. And, of course, right from the outset in funboard surfing you need to find a technique which is as energy-saving as possible.

The illustrations on the right-hand page show Robby Naish in various positions. Note his body position, developed over thousands of hours of hard practice on the water while using the least energy possible. It is typified as follows:

- Arms full stretch.
- Mast hand using reverse grip.
- Hands shoulder-width apart.
- Leaning a long way out to windward.

When sailing an up-wind course, this is the correct positioning of the body on the board. Picture 1: position in a normal wind. Picture 2: when there is too little wind, either place yourself by the mast (left) or shift your bodyweight forward (right).

Crouching to cushion the effect of the waves (picture 3).

1

2

3

Arms at full stretch, forward foot braced to the front of the board.

- ○ Spine slightly flexed, never straight or concave.
- ○ Bracing of the forward and sideways forces by the slightly-bent forward leg.
- ○ Rear leg more bent, and essentially not supporting the bodyweight, but used for steering and stabilizing.
- ○ Even when sailing up-wind courses, the body twisted slightly towards the front.

Your position on the board should never be stiff, and this is in any case quite impossible in wave conditions. Your body should be flexible enough to respond to anything. Just as a skier evens out bumps in the ground, in windsurfing you are constantly using your whole body to react to the wind and the water. Your foot position determines correct trim. If you stand too far forward in any great wind, you are in the wrong

Body turned slightly forwards, mast hand using reverse grip, upper body leaned backwards.

position to surf at your best. On the other hand, in a light wind you will turn the stern into a brake if you stand too far back.

Thanks to mast tracks, you can nowadays regulate the correct position in relation to the rig. These are normally the correct positions:

- ○ Tacking; forward position (board has its full length in the water).
- ○ For speed on courses from up-wind to broad-reach: rear position. (Smaller wet surfaces, best possibilities of gliding.)
- ○ Maneuver-surfing: middle to rear position.

Speed surfing: both feet on the stern.

The 360° turn on a sinker, one of the most difficult funboard maneuvers. (Clockwise from bottom right).

The "360"

6

7

The 360-degree turn has probably been familiar to you since your earliest hours of instruction. You luff up, keep the sail taut, and make the board turn a full circle. However, one of the toughest maneuvers is a 360 on a short funboard, where instead of luffing up, you bear away, just as on a jibe, and then glide through 360 degrees following a constant curve.

We have already described the knees-bent weighting on the leeward edge in the various jibe forms. This turn begins in a similar way:

- ○ You bear away using foot steering. For this you stand well forward on your short funboard, so that the board gathers more speed into the turn.
- ○ Now don't incline the sail to the wind any more, but instead tip it inwards, just as with a duck jibe. However, this time hold it with both hands on the boom, until it is about a meter above the water.
- ○ With your weight as far inwards as you can get it, steer the board on an even tighter curve.
- ○ Meanwhile the position of the sail, which previously had been pushed to leeward, has changed so much that you now haul it back. The wind tries to blow it upright (picture 4).
- ○ You take advantage of this, stand upright with the sail, haul in tight, and start rig steering to bear away (picture 5).
- ○ The sinker is brought away from its standstill, helped by you hanging from the sail, which lightens the board and helps it reach its planing phase more quickly (picture 6).

The critical point of the 360 turn is reached after about halfway. If there is not sufficient initial speed, or the turn is too sharp, the board slows up and sinks, and the sail, already bent sharply over, touches the water. The boom-end starts to drag, either acting as a brake or deflecting the course, which ends the turning movement. Only repeated practice helps here.

The higher the speed to start with, the better are the chances of being also to get to the point where the sail starts to lift itself up from its almost flat position relative to the water. Make user you have the correct position, so that at rest the board is well balanced.

Freestyle

Freestyle has been one of the most popular variants since windsurfing began. But in recent years the advent of funboards and the tendency towards professionalism has almost made freestyle a thing of the past.

When Hoyle Schweitzer and Jim Drake built the Original Windsurfer in 1969, they would not have given much thought to the developments which would stem from it. Nor, probably, did Newman Darby, who had already built a sailboard in 1965 and had sold blueprints for making them. Even now, boardsailing is still an experimental field, and we cannot guess at what developments will take place.

First, there was the deveolpment to large-volume regatta boards, followed by the reverse development towards tiny wave-riding boards. Somewhere in between lies a compromise. There must be a board with enough volume which still can be fun when there is hardly any wind. With such a board, freestyle—or hotdogging as it is also called—could become fashionable again.

It is very frustrating for an ambitious sailor if he is stuck on the shore with his little sinker, just yearning for the wind to get up sufficiently. With a big board he would be in his element right from force 2 or 3. In such a wind, sailing hither and thither gradually loses its appeal, and tricks and maneuvers which can be built up to ever-increasing levels of difficulty come into their own.

What exactly is freestyle? Freestyle is still part of the official one-design-class world championships of the International Yard Racing Union (IYRU). Just as in ice skating, a jury gives points for the performance of certain figures. Inside a laid-out area on the water the sailor follows his own course, performing as many difficult maneuvers as possible within a given time limit. It starts with a simple 360-degree turn, and goes on to tricks such as rolling around the boom, or standing on the edge of the board within the boom and surfing backwards. There are no limits to the inventions and the tricks. The rig can even be separated from the board, put on your head or held between your feet. Freestyle sailing is the blending of happy games with wind and waves.

You can carry out the widest range of tricks in a comparatively light wind. And, of course, practicing freestyle increases your skills of balance and your reactions, which all goes to improve your normal sailing. Above all, it improves your stance on the board.

Freestyle is not just a matter of carrying out exact maneuvers. Trick surfers attach most importance to the control of the board through harmonious movements of the body. Positions are changed and stances adopted that produce visually appealing movements. In particular, changes of position from the fully stretched to the deeply bowed, lightning turns, beautifully cushioned jumps and precision handholds are what sailing is all about.

The right board

The best freestyle boards have a large capacity, perhaps 230 – 260 liters (60¾ – 68⅔ gal) volume. They should have no sharp edges, and be known for a particularly stable ride. Of course, some tricks can be carried out on small boards, but you are always dependent on getting a stronger wind. The sail should be 5 m^2 to 6 m^2 (53¾ – 64½) in area. The boom can be somewhat longer, just like the one originally provided with all windsurfers.

247

Preparing for a simple exercise

Follow the series of pictures from left to right. Bearing away from a beam-reach course to a running course, use sail steering to turn the stern through the wind, and keep turning without shifting sail until you come on to a downwind course. Let go with the sail hand, and, while the sail is shifting, turn your body through a full circle, sailing facing the stern for a short time in the process.

Now turn the sail through 180 degrees, using the intermediate grip on the sail foot. Then surf with the clew to the wind, and next turn the sail through 180 degrees again, during which the body moves in front of the mast, facing the sail. Now work out for yourself how to get back into a normal position!

The jibe with a daggerboard

In trick surfing, the daggerboard almost always stays down, even when jibing. So we shall show you again the maneuver which forms the basis of many freestyle figures.

- Bear away using sail steering.
- Step back on the stern and clearly put your weight on the outer side of the board firmly. (In pictures 2 and 3 the surfer is lifting the other foot, so the whole body weight comes on the outside.)
- Pull the mast right back, and swing the sail around hard.

Sailing with your back to the sail, and to windward

This is a simple exercise to start with, slipping inside the boom on a beam-reach course. Once you have found the correct angle for the sail, turn yourself through 180 degrees and surf with your back to the sail.

Surfing in the boom, with your back to the sail.

1

2

3

Doing the splits on the board, an attractive maneuver which demands a great sense of balance and control of the rig.

Doing the splits on the board

On a broad-reach course you set the feet wide apart and bend forward, so that you hold the mast with the mast hand and the sail-foot with the sail hand. You let yourself slide down the mast gradually as you do the splits. The feet (picture 2) follow the board's center line. In this position you can jibe through sail shifting (picture 3).

A 360-degree turn from windward to leeward

In an up-wind position you turn yourself at lightning speed through 360 degrees in front of the mast and on the leeward side of the sail. While you are turning, take a quick hold on the rig to stop it toppling over. This trick needs a lot of practice, and of course is only possible on a big board with the necessary stability.

Pirouette on a running course

Get on to a running course, and stabilize the sail with its center of gravity right above the mast-foot. It should not be able to topple either to right or left. Now let go and turn through 360 degrees on one foot. In a light wind you do this trick quite fast.

A 360° turn before the mast, and a pirouette on a broad-reach course.

Picture sequence above:
A way of turning the sail which has a high degree of difficulty. A duck jibe, then a 180-degree turn with the sail. Changing grip to mast and sail-foot, and a further 180° turn of the sail. (Left to right).

Turning the sail through 180° from a leeward position against the wind. (Left to right).

Top sequence:
Setting the board on its edge—a popular maneuver which can also be carried out from the lee side of the sail—known as railriding.

Middle sequence:
Surfing backwards, and at the same time putting the board on its edge, demands a high degree of balance and control of the rig. You can see the way the board is put in position by the "grip" of the feet. Standing on the edge of the board, you can slip inside the boom on the windward side.

Suddenly standing on the stern and thus making the board adopt a vertical position (left) or using the rig with the mast-foot uppermost (right)—two favorite freestyle maneuvers.

Speed sailing

One reason for the great success of funboard surfing is the incredible speed these small boards can reach. If even the beginner, getting his all-around board moving for the first time, can be inspired by his speed, it's quite understandable that advanced surfers can do 40 kph (22 knots) or more on their sinkers.

The fascination is not just in the speed itself, but the experience of handing apparently without effort from the harness, gliding over the water, and feeling the splash of the spray. It gives you the motivation to go faster and faster.

The industry quickly recognized this need, and produced a plethora of speed boards, speed fins, speed

rigs and aerodynamically designed surf suits. Sails in particular have brought the manufacturer good profits. The construction of sails, masts and booms is becoming more and more complicated. The necessary materials have become increasingly expensive, with the result that the modern rig can now cost more than a good board.

It is clear, of course, that a stiff mast and long battens, which give the sail a semi-rigid profile, are far better for high speed than the unbattened sails of the past. However, it is doubtful whether you need go to the lengths of having an elliptical mast profiled profile mast pocket, or even a rigid-profile sail. Even at "speed weeks," where high-speed

Speed-surfing, a fascinating experience.

enthusiasts get together to break the world record, you regularly find, in the top five, sailors who use normal production sails.

The speed board

In order to get up to high speeds, short, narrow boards are used, the so-called "guns." According to the weight of the sailor, these are between 2.2 and 3.0 m (7 – 9¾ ft) long, and between 45 and 55 cm (18 – 22 in) wide. The most important area is right towards the rear, because the board needs good planing characteristics. This means its underwater hull can have differing forms. Some swear by concave surfaces at the front, and a shallow V-shape to the rear, while others go for wingers, which have gently downward-sloping "wings" giving concave surfaces at the stern. In any case, we are talking about smooth, swept-back shapes to the rear of the board.

1

2

You can go fast on speed slalom boards and still have good maneuvering capabilities (picture 1). Both feet on the stern of a gun (picture 2). Similarly on a long race board (picture 3). The technique is to have the mast track right back, so that only the rear part of the board is actually in contact with the water.

The "body-drag" (also pictured right). On a broad-reach course suddenly jump off sideways and let your body drag in the water, finally jumping back on again.

The technique of speed-surfing

Slide the mast right back in its track. Set your harness lines long enough for you to sail with your arms almost at full stretch. On medium funboards put both feet in the rear set of footstraps. However, this is not imperative, and certainly isn't correct for short funboards.

The main principle is to have as little friction resistance between board and water as possible. For this reason you have to cut down the wetted surface of the underwater hull. You can see this clearly in the picture of Robby Naish. Although the board he is using is 3.55 m (11⅔ ft) long, he is gliding literally on the last meter of it. This is why he is using the stern foot straps.

Make sure you keep the board horizontal in the water, tipping it neither to windward nor to leeward. Keep your bodyweight well back, because an upright stance, which in a strong wind is more difficult anyway, can lead to bad crashes when the bow, which would then have more weight on it, cuts under the water and causes a sudden jolt. If you lean well back, you stop the braking effect of the bow.

If you want to find out just how fast you go, first pick out a test stretch where you won't be likely to bother anyone. In any case, make sure you are always in full control of your board, even in extreme situations. Unfortunately, you do get speed fanatics who have their private speed battles close inshore and are in no state to yield right of way, or to react quickly enough to dangerous situations.

One-hand jibe at high speed, with a head dip, letting your head touch the water. These belong to speed surfing.

The problem of spin-out

A spin-out at high speed can be dangerous, with the board suddenly turning or slipping sideways and you and the rig being thrown diagonally forward. But it has been shown that by correctly diverting some of the force of the wind from the sail over your feet onto the board you can generally avoid spin-outs. Especially when you are crossing small waves and the stern comes out of the water for an instant, you can minimize this effect when you re-enter the water by countering the sideways force which you can feel on the fins through your feet. (See spin-out, page 12.)

Windsurfing racing

A small but growing number of sailors want to measure how good they are in races. The original triangular regatta course, borrowed from yacht racing, has been considerably modified and, one could say, restyled for windsurfing. For in racing you can do a lot more with the windsurfer than with a traditional sailing boat, whose crew plays a basically passive role apart from when they are trapeze sailing.

With the windsurfer, the physical contribution plays a major part. For this reason, windsurfer racers don't just want to follow a set course around a few buoys; they prefer to choose events in which technique, tactics and control of the board are of paramount importance. This is the way that the single class of the International Yacht Racing Union has gone, along with the Triangle Regatta Buoy Races, the freestyle organizations and the so-called Long Distance Races. There are also a considerable number of funboard events, right up to the professional World Cup, which are made up of several disciplines. The World Cup events came through a democratic meeting of organizers and competitors. They represent the ultimate in surfing competition.

Course racing

The course race can be compared to the traditional triangular course sailing regatta. In order to make it tougher, though, a buoy slalom is added, and the remainder of the course includes as much close-reach and broad-reach work as possible, which ensures high speed. Endless zigzag tacking legs, which are no fun and only tire you out, are avoided in favor of the courses which promote tactical skills and the clever use of wind changes.

The races take place only if the wind is above a given strength, thus avoiding light-wind situations in which a sudden gust out of a calm might provide a chance winner.

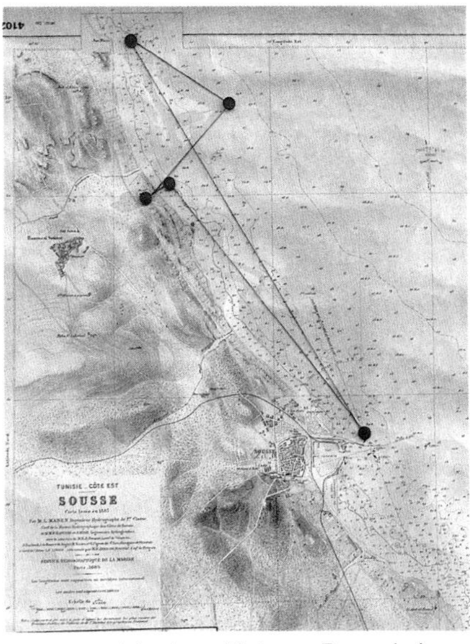

The map of the Long Distance Race, during an official one-design world championship of the IYRU.

In-and-out

A further type of competition is a speed race between two buoys, which are so placed as to ensure that you have to keep crossing the surf. Preferably, you go out against the surf, and come back with it on a beam-reach or broad-reach course, hence the name "in-and-out." Depending on the number of competitors in the event, between four and eight sailors take part in each run. A knock-out system operates, so that the best of each group qualify for the next round.

This kind of event has provoked the development of a special type of board, the so-called slalom board, which has also proved ideal for much normal windsurfing.

Wave-riding

In the third type of competition for the World Cup, competitors show their worth on small boards in the surf. Here it is not only the ability to ride the waves that counts, but also maneuvers like the duck jibe, the 360, acrobatic jumps, and so on.

Just as in freestyle competitions, each surfer is allowed a given time. His performance is observed by a jury. All three disciplines are rated on a points scale, which then produces a world or European champion.

Buoy slaloms

The illustration above shows a typical buoy slalom course for a world championship. Start and finish are on the right of the picture (1). Normally a group of between four and six sailors compete at a time, on a knock-out system. Starting on an extremely close-hauled course (2) they reach the first buoy (3). After the turn they come back on a broad-reach course to the start buoy. Now the true slalom begins, which has to be tackled one way against the wind and the other with the wind behind.

First you must zigzag (5), then take a fast beam-reach course to the first

The group at the start (position 1 above).

Going around the big turn marker (position 3); Zigzag around the small markers (position 5).

The complete course for a buoy slalom.

buoy. From then on, more beam-reach work until you round the far buoy, and come back, jibing around every mark until the finish.

Events like this are thrilling, because the spectators can see everything happening virtually underneath their noses. As with the World Cup, the course for buoy races are laid out right by the shore. A great deal of care is taken to choose stretches of coastline and bays where there is a relatively high chance of the right wind level.

In the case of courses like the one described, not only mastery of the board is needed, but also a good level of tactical know-how. The slalom course, for instance, ensures a lot of overtaking, which is difficult to do without breaking the rules. You have to wait for just the right moment. For this reason, sailors are often neck and neck, which makes for real race excitement. In this kind of race you hardly ever get a favorite out in front from start to finish unchallenged.

Pursuit race on the zigzag stretch.

Tight jibe on the way back to the finish.

Maneuvers around the buoys

It is interesting to follow the maneuvers around buoys. You have the choice of reducing your speed to just get around the buoy, or taking a bigger arc and keeping up your speed. However, the bigger arc means covering more distance. The essence of races of this kind lies in choosing between the two solutions. Of course there are often collisions around the turns, so you have to allow a safety margin around them.

Your stance on the board is vital. If you are just a few centimeters away from where your bodyweight should be, either the board won't accelerate as it should, or you will be left trying to brake when on a fast broad-reach course.

In-and-out

This kind of race is especially attractive, so let us take another look at it.

In-and-outs are spectacular races between two buoys. They are spectacular because the course crosses the surf line. Soon after the start the wheat is separated from the chaff. Who will cross the waves, which at times are a meter high? Naturally no one wants to lose speed, so there is bound to be wave-jumping, and jumping for distance rather than height. The return run is just as difficult, for here the waves have to be ridden. How to get back to the buoy which lies close to the shore? The spectators are a mere glance away from the action. When the competitors pass the land buoy they are immediately inspired again. Within and outside the surf zone there is the added excitement of attempts to pass. The buoys have to be rounded several times, but the whole race is run off at such a tempo that just one fall or a bad maneuver around a buoy is enough to cost victory.

The boards used are the short slalom boards described on page 8. Different sails are used, depending on the wind, and any size of sail is permitted. Naturally, races only take place if there is enough wind, which guarantees really high speed. The

1

2

Jumping through the surf line at high speed.

Chasing the leader on the way back to the inner buoy.

The battle of the sails. Each competitor must have several rigs prepared for changing wind conditions.

mark of the expert is the way he rounds the buoys, jibing every time. This highly-competitive way of rounding is often referred to as the "carve jibe." The body is leaned far forward and the board tipped inwards. The board is virtually put on one long edge, which works as a kind of rudder. The opposite to this would be to push the stern right down to give a tight jibe turn, but this would mean a loss of speed. With a carve jibe you would choose a relatively greater arc around the buoy but at high speed. The idea is to start the arc early, and aim to shave the buoy as you round it.

▼ Women, too, surf in the World Cup. They make up for the male strength advantage with good balance and a delicate touch.

▼ Taking a long jump over small waves.

With beginners, you often see them start their jibe arc too late, and they have too much to spare around the buoy, which means a longer run to the next mark. If you are to succeed, it is important that you ride the waves well on the run back towards the shore. If you don't catch a wave just right, you can find someone else from a worse position suddenly passing you on the right wave. This is where you really get the most exciting jockeying for positions. If the wave isn't running parallel to the shoreline, but at an angle, you can see the experts spotting it, and suddenly departing from the straight line between the buoys in order to pick up a wave coming at a better angle, and thus get to the buoy more quickly.

Naturally, the ability to take the wind from your opponent's sail can sometimes play its part. Although there are usually only between four and eight competitors at a time, you can use clever tactics to take the wind. So right after every buoy you try to keep to windward.

On almost all stretches of coast which are used for this type of competition, there are, to a greater or lesser degree, currents to contend with. You have to take the drift of the current into account for your tactical plans.

Choice of sail plays a big part, too. The sail profile must be set up for maximum efficiency. There is no room for poor sail trim: tight sail for strong wind and slack sail for light wind. So a professional surfer will take along to a race all sorts of sails, with sizes covering every half square meter. Just before the start, there are frenzied calculations as to which size of sail is the right one. Miscalculate, and, whether it is too large or too small, you have lost before the start. Too large a sail brings as many disadvantages as too small a one. With too large a sail you can't judge things precisely, and you have to keep on slackening it. In many cases, surfers with smaller sails do better.

So there are many factors which influence this race, even though it is simply around two buoys.

The buoys are placed to give the maximum beam-reach work, and hence high speed.

▲
Coming back through the surf, the waves are used as an additional drive. With luck and correct steering on the wave crests you can gain a good lead over your pursuers.

◄
Through tight jibing you give away no ground at the turn marker.

Safety in funboard-surfing

Funboard sailing can mean getting yourself into extreme situations. There are waves and surf, of course; but, above all, danger lurks for surfers in strong, often offshore winds on exposed coastline. Bad accidents, generally speaking, have nothing to do with equipment failure, but can always be traced back to mistakes on the part of the sailors. Windsurfing as a sport is not dangerous if you practice it correctly. This is why windsurfing schools and instructors must carry on their work to spread the gospel of well-tried and worthwhile rules which protect the surfer from endangering himself or injuring others.

So carefully note this advice:

- Test board and rig before every outing. Do a specially careful check of the mast-foot joint, the major lines and their knots, as well as the mast, boom and sail.
- Especially with small surfboards, as a matter of principle tie rig and board together with a safety line. In strong winds light boards are so quickly swept away that it is often impossible for even the strongest swimmer to recover them.
- In high winds, only use a sail which you can control.
- Wear comprehensive protective clothing against the cold. Even in the warm seasons, protect your lower back and your feet with foam rubber.
- If you are sailing in unfamiliar waters, collect the following specific information: current, any sudden winds, special weather peculiarities, and so on.
- In principle, don't sail alone on the coast. Above all, don't go into the water alone in strong offshore winds. This very important rule has been frequently disregarded in the past, with the result of costly rescue operations and even death.
- On a windsurfing trip you must report out and report back. Make sure you tell a responsible person when and from where you are leaving, where you are going, and when you expect to be back.
- On coastal waters or on estuaries wear, as a matter of principle, a harness with a buoyancy vest. At least part of your clothing should be light-colored.
- If you change from an all-around funboard to a smaller, faster board, don't revel in the high speed straight away. First practice your foot steering.
- Sail carefully in crowded waters. No spectacular maneuvers!
- Basically keep 100 meters out from the shore. Be wary of any bathing or swimming places. Keep a lookout, even far out, for swimmers and snorkel-divers.
- Respect all nature reserves, keep shorelines and beaches clean, and place your board and rig where it will not restrict access to and from the water for other sailors.
- Contribute, through exemplary following of the rules of right of way, to a well-ordered co-existence with other water-sport participants.
- If you don't know these rules, make sure you find a sailing school and get the necessary instruction. Apart from this, it does no harm to look out for a place of instruction, where you can get a quick, safe course on everything to do with funboard-sailing.
- When surfing on the coast, take with you the following rescue aids:
  Buoyancy harness or life vest.
  Safety and towing lines.
  Rescue flares.
  Extensive warm clothing.
  Replacement mast-foot joint.
  Replacement lines.
  Sticky tape.

Windsurfing the breakers

In this chapter we shall give you a fascinating glimpse into the tremendous possibilities of using small boards in the waves. We shall show you how to ride the waves, and to use them as a launch ramp. In the waves themselves, and in the troughs between them, you can carry out high-speed maneuvers that for skill and sheer daredevilry can hardly be beaten.

Windsurfing was born in the waves, and the experts are drawn back towards this birthplace. The waves enhance quite considerably the sport of windsurfing. Whereas on flat water you are dependent on the drive of the sail, with waves you can achieve far greater speeds than would be possible under "sail power" alone. Surfing the breakers means using the sail principally for cutting across the waves or for jumping up out of them.

Once back in the waves, the sail is really only used for steering, because in the incredible downhill runs off the wave crests you develop so much speed that the sail itself becomes ineffective, or sometimes even a hindrance.

In the surf area you must watch the cycle of the waves.

Starting from the shore

Usually an attempt to start from the shore ends in a fiasco with the first waves. The board, before it hardly gets going, is taken by the water, whipped sideways, and suddenly you find yourself deposited back on dry land again, quite often with a few bruises. A beach start into surf may look easy, but it is a matter of practicing the exact moves.

Go right up to the water's edge with your board (the carrying technique is described on page 28), and look at the way the waves are forming. Give yourself plenty of time for this. After the wave has run out onto the beach, there is always a pause, which is long enough to do a beach start in shallow water. It is difficult in an onshore wind, because this means you have to sail away at an angle to the waves, and that is when the danger of being thrown back in again is at its greatest.

The pictures on the right show wrong handling in the surf area. The boards are turned sideways by the waves and thrown backwards. You can see the correct method in the sequence below. The bow is always pointed in the direction of the wave.

Watch out for the extensive area of foaming surf, which is created when the wave has broken, and stays as a carpet of boiling water between the wave crests near the shore. If you hit this area at good speed, you will suddenly feel a braking effect, and you could find yourself going head over heels into the water. You have to make sure that your bow reaches this surf zone at the correct angle. Shift your bodyweight briefly to the stern, ease the impact of the surf by slackening sail for a short time, then immediately tighten sail again and shift your weight forward. In an onshore wind you will bear away again and pick up speed.

1

2

3

Beaching correctly needs quick reactions and correct control of the board.

Crossing the waves is a matter of skill and daring.

Beach start: the right position in relation to the waves

As soon as you get into the water, the bow must be pointing towards the waves. If the angle is even slightly wrong, then the board will be turned sideways by the force of the water, and the board thrown back onto the beach (pictures at the top of the page). Then you will just have to wait until the next break in the waves before you can start again.

Pictures 1,2 and 3 show the correct positioning. Turning the sail (with your mast hand as necessary on the mast) you bring the board to the right angle to the incoming wave. From this position you can afford to take your time. If a wave breaks far enough out, you can start off at good speed and make for it.

Beaching

When coming in, watch what is happening to the waves on the shore. Often the water suddenly pulls back, and you find yourself abruptly running aground on the sand, which can often cause bad falls and damage to your gear. In a World Cup event, Jill Boyer shows correct beaching technique.

- Surf into the sand zone (picture 1).
- As the last of the water pulls back, run alongside the board and push it clear of the surf zone (picture 2).
- Bring the sail and board into the right position and carry the board onto dry land (picture 3).

Crossing surf-waves

When you are dealing with short, steep waves, which break violently, you often find yourself using all your strength against the roll of the surf. The most important element is keeping your weight on the back foot, and the bow straight into the wave.

Jumping over waves

Once again it is Jill Boyer showing us how to handle critical situations in the surf zone near the beach, using fast and decisive handling.

There, because of the constant carpet of foam rolling on to the beach, there is such a braking effect that you have to resort to a water start. In an instant, before the next wave starts to cause trouble, you get the board moving and cross the small incoming wave with good speed (picture 5). The next foaming carpet is already building up further out, and will have to be surmounted (background of picture 6).

In order to gain momentum you bear away somewhat and then go full speed forwards (picture 6). Now you take a moment to assess the approaching breaker. Go straight for it at speed, and cross it with a jump (pictures 7 and 8). Using a jump technique is the only way of crossing this kind of wave. (For jump techniques refer to page 114.)

1

2

3

4

5

8

7

6

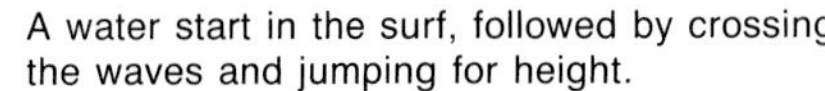

A water start in the surf, followed by crossing the waves and jumping for height.

Riding the waves

Windsurfing developed originally from surf-riding, which has a long tradition on the coast of Hawaii.

Whereas on flat water you have only the wind-strength to power your "motor sail," when it comes to wave surfing, you have in addition the speed of the wave itself and the downward slope of the wave at the front. So the sailor has three energy sources at his disposal, if used correctly:

- The wind strength, harnessed through the sail.
- The speed of the advancing wave.
- The acceleration off the overhang of the wave.

Wave-riding is therefore not just surfing off wave crests, but also the constantly changing use of the possible forces involved to drive the board. It is not just a question of using the sail perfectly, but above all of the art of wave-riding, which is the exact steering of the board by shifting bodyweight and by using foot pressure. Foot steering is used just as in calm water, but with the very significant addition of the use of bodyweight in various positions.

You often find yourself surfing the waves diagonally, and using the resultant centrifugal forces which would surely produce a fall in flat water, but on wave-mountains can

Riding the waves in a cross-wind or a diagonal offshore wind is the best practice for beginners.

be harnessed as a useful element in intricate maneuvers such as the roller coaster or the figure=eight.

Maneuvers in the waves

Try yourself out in small waves to begin with, and learn there the maneuvers which will be necessary for the biggest waves. The best conditions for this are a diagonally offshore wind or a cross-wind. In onshore winds there is the danger that the wave can become a wall between the wind and your sail, and completely destroy your maneuverability and sail power.

In addition, it isn't easy to get out through the surf zone. The best way to familiarize yourself with your first wave is to surf diagonally off them, using a kind of slalom technique off the forward side of the wave.

Bottom turn

This maneuver consists of turning back into the wave, and is similar to

1

2

Bottom turn (picture 1), cut-back (picture 2), diagonal climb towards the wave crest (picture 3), and making for the next bottom turn (picture 4).

the start of a power jibe. Lean forward a little, so that your bodyweight is over your bent legs, and maneuver the board into a curve using the pressure of the balls of your feet, principally the back foot. In an offshore wind you bear away in the direction of the wave. The sail is pulled tight, so that you move diagonally up the wave.

The curve of this maneuver, like that of a jibe on flat water, can be either of a wide radius or, using bodyweight to the rear and heavy foot steering by tipping the board to leeward, can be of a tighter radius.

Cut-back

Once you have done a bottom turn and, through sailing diagonally upwards, have once again reached the crest, the cut-back takes you back down again. This is a radical altering of course, a steering maneuver which comes about exclusively through foot steering and weight transference. The difficulty, after the bottom turn and the diagonal progress upwards, is to come suddenly out of the forward-bent and somewhat crouched position into a laid-back stance, so that the necessary bodyweight can come over the back foot, which can then steer the edge of the board. So you have to go from leeward-leaning forward position (bottom turn) into a windward-leaning rear position (cut-back). A radical cut-back would certainly lead to a spin-out on flat water. But in waves you can push the stern well down to obtain grip.

The most extreme form of this maneuver is to use the foaming crest of the breaking wave. After the bottom turn you traverse the wave at such an angle that you reach its crest just as it is beginning to break.

At speed you now start to curve against the breaking wave, which wraps around the board and takes it down the face again. This is called a cut-back "off the lip."

Jibing "off the lip"

You can also do some good, tight jibes against a wave.

N.B.:
- Surf up to the breaking part of the wave.
- Briefly slacken sail and bear away using foot steering.
- While you are in the "white water" the mast hand holds the mast.
- Surf down the wave and then sail.

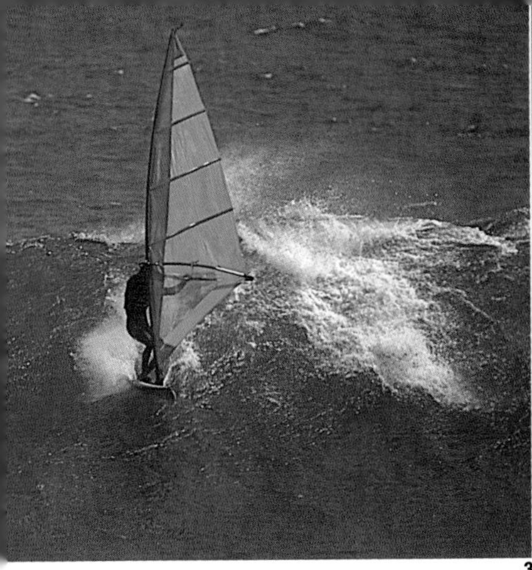

3

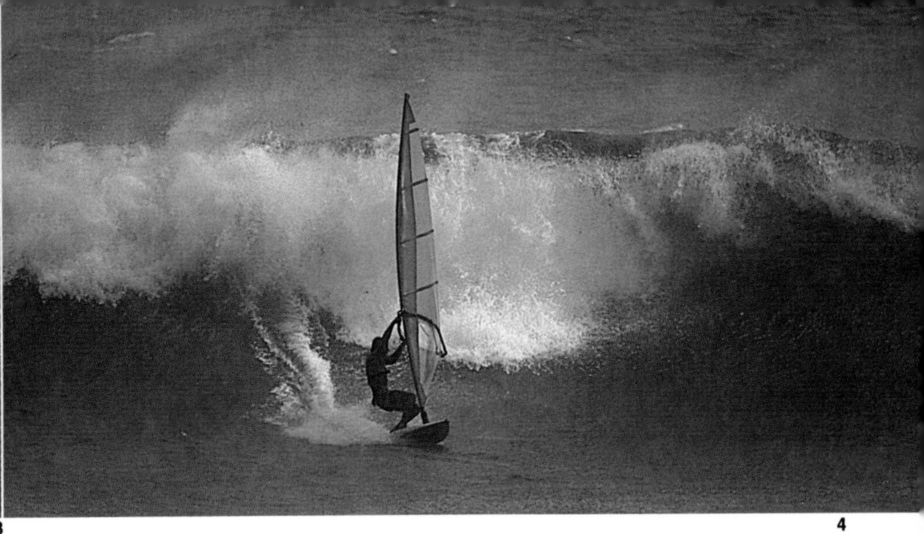

4

1 2 3 4

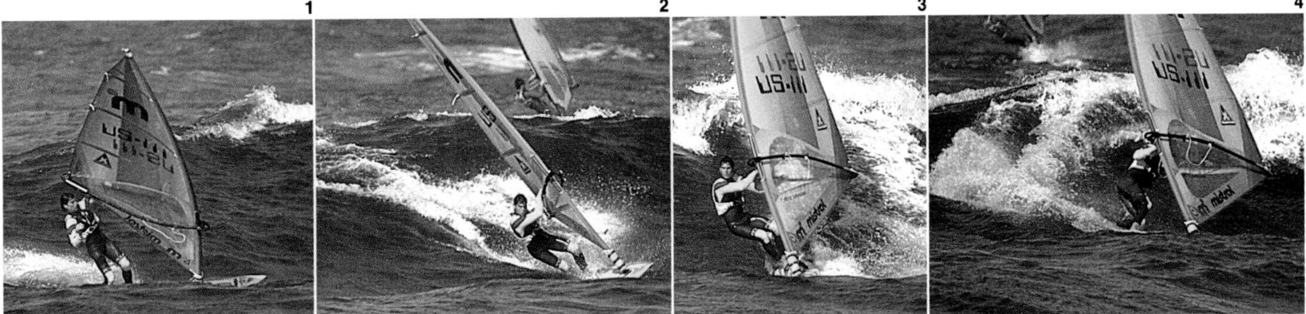

▲ Wave maneuvers: duck jibe on the wave face (picture 1), riding down the wave (pictures 2 and 3), and back to the bottom turn (picture 4).

▼ The "off the lip" jibe.

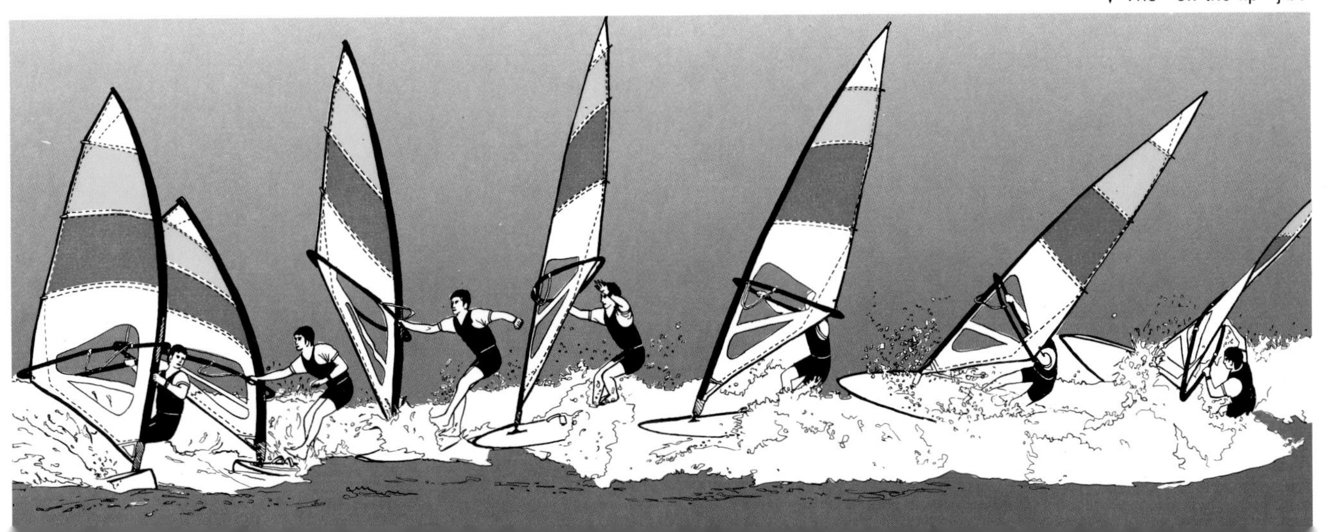

Bottom turn (picture 2), cut-back (picture 3), riding down (picture 4), duck jibe on the wave face (picture 5), cut-back (picture 6), and wave-traversing (picture 7).

Sail maneuvers and wave-riding

On calm water you must always pick up speed with the sail so as to tackle certain maneuvers like the duck jibe or the 360, which need a high initial speed. When you are wave-riding, you have the necessary high speed after a fast wave descent. This allows you to carry out good sail maneuvers. But of course, the degree of difficulty is a lot higher than on flat water, because you haven't much time, and only a little margin for error.

3
4
6
7

Wave jumping

You can use a wave as a springboard. Not just the big breakers, but even the smallest swell is enough to give you lift-off. It really isn't too difficult.

Sail your funboard on beam-reach, so that you are moving across the direction of the swell-waves. At maximum speed look out for a little wave "hill" that might serve as your springboard, luff up sharply, and, with your front foot in the strap, pull up on the bow, which will let you sail diagonally across the wave. Keep the sail tight, and as soon as the stern reaches the top of the wave you pull the board up by bending your legs. This is how you manage a small "hop." The stronger the wind, and the more effort you put into your take-off, the higher and farther you will jump, even in calm water.

With bigger and longer funboards you can even use the hull of the board as a wind-break. You jump from a wave in the direction of the true wind, which deflects you in mid-air, and you land on a broad-reach course.

In the breakers wave-jumping is easier, but landing is a lot more difficult. Above all, do not practice jumping at maximum speed, but at a controlled speed, and landing with the stern first. There used to be wider stern-shapes, which made stern-first landings more difficult, and even led to boards breaking. With present-day slim pintails the stern sinks in deep and cushions the impact of the board on the surface of the water.

Start with smaller waves, and choose a place where the crest hasn't yet started to break. First bear away from the wave to pick up the necessary speed, then luff up again, so that you meet the wave crest at the correct angle. Pull the nose of the board up again with your foot in

the forward strap, and slacken sail slightly. At first, take things gently, so that you just clear the top of the wave and glide down the other side. If you were really to keep the sail tight and go full tilt, you would shoot far out over the wave, and this could lead to a fall. It is far better to try to sail tighter and tighter with each successive jump, so that you go gradually farther and higher.

It is also worthwhile in wave-jumping to suddenly bend your legs so as to pull the stern up. And during the "flight phase" try to stabilize your board in a horizontal position.

Jumping for height, with simultaneous sideways turning of the board—the donkey-kick.

▲ Jumping for height.

Jumping for distance. ►

High jumps

For high jumps the wind should be blowing parallel to the beach or be cross-offshore. There should be some good, steep waves. Get up to top speed, and shoot up them vertically. Shortly after the jump you push the board over sideways, which makes the sail point downwards, hence the name "upside-down." Usually the top of the sail touches the wave's white-water crest. During the jump slacken sail, and on landing pull in again, giving a parachute effect.

In jumps aimed at height it can of course happen that you can't complete the turning process in time to land the board right-side up. It is then better to bail out, or at least to pull your feet out of the straps. Experts hang on to the boom until

▲ Jumping into the dizzy heights. When you consider that the sailor jumps from one wave crest and lands in the following wave trough, you realize that we are talking of daredevil acrobatics, where height differences are often between 5 and 10 meters.

◄ Jumping for height upside-down. You jump vertically upwards from the steepest part of the wave, then twist the board sideways and finally bring it above your head, the tip of the sail touching the water. You naturally need enough height to give you room to bring the board back underneath your body again.

their body touches the water, thus using the sail as a parachute to slow descent.

Jumping for distance

If you are jumping for distance, the waves do not need to be so steep. But it is important to approach them at maximum speed. Slightly lift the bow, and then immediately pull the stern up high. Afterwards the legs stay quite bent. You seem, in fact, to be sitting on the board. The sail is flattened parallel to the board. You can land with the bow slightly downwards, but it is important that you take the impact on your feet, particularly with the front foot stretched out, so you are not thrown forward. Landing with the bow downwards needs great care, and is much more dangerous than a stern landing.

When jumping for height the sail is used in the landing like a wing.

Pictured on facing page:
In jumping for distance you keep the sail tight, for additional drive.